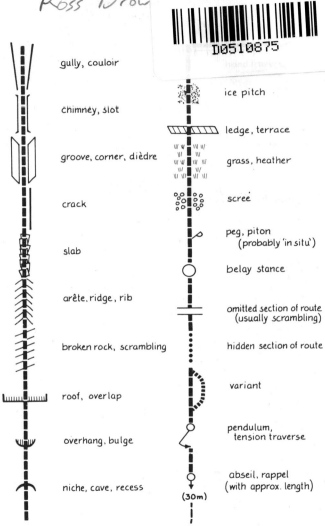

gully, couloir

chimney, slot

groove, corner, dièdre

crack

slab

arête, ridge, rib

broken rock, scrambling

roof, overlap

overhang, bulge

niche, cave, recess

ice pitch

ledge, terrace

grass, heather

scree

peg, piton
(probably 'in situ')

belay stance

omitted section of route
(usually scrambling)

hidden section of route

variant

pendulum,
tension traverse

abseil, rappel
(with approx. length)

(30m)

SCOTLAND

Central and Southern Highlands

Ken Crocket and Steve Ashton

The Crowood Press

First published in 1988 by
The Crowood Press
Ramsbury, Marlborough,
Wiltshire SN8 2HE

British Library Cataloguing in Publication Data
Crocket, Ken, *1948 —*
    Scotland : Central and Southern Highlands.
    ——(100 classic climbs).
    1. Scotland. Highlands. Mountains - for
    climbing
    I. Title   II. Ashton, Steve   III. Series
    796.5'22

    ISBN 1 – 85223 – 025 – 8

Cover photographs by Ken Crocket

*Front: Alastair Walker on the exit from Summit Gully (Route 56), Stob Coire
nam Beith, Glencoe.*

Back: Climbers on Sou'Wester Slabs (Route 4), Cir Mhor, Arran.

Typeset by Action Typesetting Limited, Gloucester.
Printed in Great Britain at the University Printing House, Oxford

Contents

Preface

This guide describes, with the aid of topo diagrams, a balanced selection of 100 routes from the varied and myriad climbs to be found in the Central and Southern Highlands of Scotland. Drawing on 20 years of personal experience, I have placed the emphasis on routes of quality, graded *Easy* to *E2* in summer, and *I* to *V* in winter. My intention here is to give a functional introduction to the climbing in these areas, both for first-time visitors, and for those who can visit but rarely.

The selection of routes was not an easy task. Along with better-known routes that are described are several that are relatively unknown, and some of these are published in a guide for the first time. The criterion for inclusion has always been climbing enjoyment, and it is hoped that there will be many pleasant surprises in the list.

Those who wish to explore the region in greater depth will find the rock and ice guides published by the Scottish Mountaineering Club to be indispensable. The SMC's annual journal is also rich in information and literature on the Scottish mountains.

Over-detailed descriptions are not provided, leaving the climber with that sense of adventure which contributes so much to the overall enjoyment. The climbs described here have been the source of much pleasure, hopefully to be shared through the medium of this guide.

Acknowledgements

We climb because we like to, and it is easy to forget the patient suffering of climbing companions who have been asked to stop for photographs on a route, often in awkward spots, or who have been pestered for photographs or memory-refreshing information. Obviously I wish to thank all those with whom I have climbed over the last two decades. In addition, the following must be mentioned with respect to the preparation of this guide: Andy Hart, Ken Moneypenny, Colin Stead and Alastair Walker.

Ken Crocket
Glasgow 1988

Introduction

The Central and Southern Highlands provide a selection of climbs as rich and varied as any that might be drawn from the entire length and breadth of Scotland.

Rock type strongly influences the character of summer routes. Represented here are both the rough and smooth granites of Arran and Glen Etive; the rippling, contorted strata of Arrochar's mica schist; and the steep, rhyolite walls of Glencoe, with their confusion of holds.

In winter, the scale and setting of the mountain tend to dominate the experience. The long ridges of Ben Nevis, and the great winter gullies and face routes of both Ben Nevis and Creag Meaghaidh, provide climbing days of alpine character. Climbs of the Southern Highlands, hitherto unfrequented despite easy access, complement these more famous outings.

It seems idyllic, but there is a price to pay. Most Scottish mountain crags are anything from one to three hours' walk from the nearest road, with a commensurate increase in altitude. The implications of this, particularly in winter, should be obvious — the equipment, clothing, and fitness of the party must be carefully considered. Navigational skills may also be called upon, especially in winter when attempting to descend from a featureless summit plateau on Ben Nevis or Creag Meaghaidh.

During the last decade, the popular winter routes of Glencoe and Ben Nevis have unfortunately become badly crowded. Helping to offset this, areas further south will often be found to be surprisingly quiet. In parts of Arran and the Southern Highlands, for instance, it is still possible to climb all day without encountering another party.

How to use the Guide

AREA INTRODUCTIONS

Routes are described under one of seven area headings: Arran, Arrochar, Southern Highlands, Glencoe, Ardgour, Ben Nevis, and Creag Meaghaidh. A brief introduction to each describes climbing typical of the area, and highlights its special qualities. Further notes identify approaches by car or public transport, and suggest where to look for accommodation. An accompanying map locates valley bases and crag approach paths.

ROUTE INFORMATION

Concise details of each route are presented under six headings:

Summary: This is a short appraisal of the route for quick reference purposes. Along with route grade and length, it tells you all you need to know when looking for ideas.

First Ascent: These names and dates, though of little immediate significance, add a historical perspective.

Best Conditions: This reference helps you to find a suitable route according to the season and prevailing weather — hot, cold, dry, or wet.

Approach: This note is intended to get you to the crag with the minimum of confusion. It provides concise information on parking, as well as on the approach route and its duration. Grid references refer to the relevant Ordnance Survey map.

Starting Point: This locates the start and fixes the beginning of the topo, from which all further directions will be taken. You should refer to the crag diagrams, or prominent features shown on the topo, if you need to confirm this position.

Descent: This note briefly describes the most common descent routes, which are also indicated on topos and crag diagrams.

ROUTE DESCRIPTIONS

The half page of 'chat' which follows summarised route information is something you might read in the campsite or pub rather than on the crag. Its purpose is to sketch in a background to the climb. Rarely will it contain information essential for route-finding — that is the role of the topo. However, if you do get badly stuck, you might find the odd clue secreted here!

TOPO DIAGRAMS

For simplicity, all routes are identified by a number from 1 to 100. These numbers are used consistently throughout the text, as well as on topos, crag diagrams, and area maps.

Topos take the place of formal route descriptions. You will be surprised how quickly you can learn to 'read' the route by interpreting these symbols. A key at the rear of the book explains what they mean. For all that, avoid falling into the trap of reading too much into each little twist and kink of the dotted line. Topos can only show the approximate line of a route, and are best used as confirmation of intuitive route-finding decisions. This is especially true in winter, when the abundance or scarcity of snow will, from week to week, alternately obscure and reveal underlying features.

A few topos serve clusters of two or three routes. Numbering makes it plain which is which. In some cases a worthwhile neighbouring route has been indicated. Absence of a number confirms that there will be no further elaboration in the text.

GRADINGS

Nothing too controversial here. Normal adjectival grades, suitably abbreviated, have been used throughout, with the addition of a *VS +* grade to ease congestion in the *VS* and *HVS* grades. Technical grades appear directly on the topos, pinpointing major difficulties. The full range of grades and the approximate international equivalents are as follows:

British Adjectival Grade		Technical	UIAA	USA
E	Easy		I	
M	Moderate		II	
D	Difficult		III −	
D +	Hard Difficult		III	
VD	Very Difficult		III +	
VD +	Hard Very Difficult		IV	
S	Severe		IV +	
S +	Hard Severe	4a, *4b*, 4c	V	5.6
VS	Very Severe	4b, *4c*, 5a	V +	5.7
VS +	Very Severe (hard)	*4c, 5a*	VI −	5.8
HVS	Hard Very Severe	4c, *5a*, 5b	VI	5.9
E1	Mild Extremely Severe	5a, *5b*, 5c	VI + /VII −	5.10a/b
E2	Extremely Severe	5b, *5c*, 6a	VII	5.10c/d

Interpreting Grades: The adjectival or overall grade takes into account the seriousness of a route, as well as its pure technical difficulty. However, the range of technical difficulties likely to be encountered at a given overall grade is limited. This range is indicated on the table, the most common grade being emphasised. The combination of adjectival and technical grade reveals a great deal about the route. Consider Bludger's Revelation (*HVS, 5a*) and the neighbouring Shibboleth (*E2, 5b*). From these particular combinations, we can assume that major technical difficulties on Bludger's Revelation will be comparatively short and safe, whereas those on Shibboleth will be prolonged and serious.

Regional Variations: Grading attempts to be consistent across all seven areas, but discrepancies remain. For instance, you may find yourself having to work a lot harder on Arran than you would at Glencoe to succeed on a route of the same grade. The unfamiliar and physical nature of Arran rock lends itself to a strenuous if safe struggle, so perhaps there is some justification. Similar arguments could be used to explain other inconsistencies. Nevertheless, it is always a good idea to drop down a grade when first visiting a new area.

Star Ratings: Star ratings to indicate route quality would have been superfluous in this guide − they are all excellent!

WINTER ROUTES

If you are contemplating winter climbing for the first time, please take advice and instruction beforehand on equipment and techniques. This guide describes only where to find the routes, not how to climb them or how to stay alive in the hostile winter environment.

Snow & Ice Conditions: Suitable conditions for winter climbing arrive as early as November, or as late as mid-December, and usually continue through to April. Major ascents have been made as late as mid-April on Ben Nevis, where extra height produces conditions more reliable than those found on lower hills. Lean periods will occur during most years, but these seldom last for more than a week or two. Their effect is more detrimental to the Southern Highlands and Glencoe than to Ben Nevis. Avalanches are a major cause of winter fatalities, as are slips by unroped walkers and climbers. Avoid climbing during, and for at least a day after, heavy snowfall, and, if in doubt, avoid gullies and snow slopes. Don't gamble with thaws — come back another day. Creag Meaghaidh has a particularly bad reputation for rapid changes in conditions.

Grading: Winter routes are identified in the contents list by a (W). They have been graded according to the familiar Scottish system:

I   Simple snow gullies, possibly including a small ice step or corniced exit. Uncomplicated ridge traverses under good conditions.
II   Snow gullies containing a few small pitches. Exposed ridges which include small rock steps and/or knife-edges.
III   Gullies containing several pitches, some of which may be long or problematical. Escapable or low-angle ice-falls (e.g. frozen stream courses). The easier buttresses.
IV   Major gullies containing several difficult pitches. Steep ice-falls of continuous difficulty. Difficult buttress routes.
V   Major gullies with additional difficulties, such as technical rock sections. Ice-falls which include long vertical sections. Hard buttress or face routes, perhaps involving serious run-outs.

In some cases a borderline grade has been allocated (e.g. *III/IV*). This is self-explanatory. All grades relate to good winter conditions, so expect dramatic increases in difficulty if these deteriorate.

Equipment: Grades assume that twin tools will be used on all but the simplest outings, and that for ice routes these will have inclined or steeply drooped picks. Special mention has usually been made when screws or deadman/buried axes are essential for belaying. Four or five pegs, and a small selection of nuts and slings, are normally carried on routes graded *III* or harder.

Other essential winter equipment includes: helmet (a must on ice-falls!), spare food/clothing for enforced bivouacs, headtorch with spare bulb and battery, survival bag, spare mitts, map, compass and first aid kit.

Timing: Monitor weather and ground conditions and set out early to get the best from Scottish winter climbing. Your reward will be smaller queues, optimum conditions, fewer benightments, and a longer life.

ACCESS

Crag approaches follow paths which are in regular use. However, there is no automatic right of access. Discretion and courtesy often succeed, unless there is stalking. In the areas described, there should be very little confrontation during the late autumn and early winter, except possibly at Binnein Shuas.

METRIC UNITS

Metric units have been used throughout. Metric OS maps justify conversion of distances and heights, while metric ropes partially excuse conversion of route lengths. Incorrigible imperialists can reconvert by adding a zero and dividing by three (e.g. 60m = 600/3 = 200ft — actual conversion slightly under 197ft). Alternatively, for a rough approximation, multiply by three and then add a bit for good measure (a tenth to be more precise).

MORE INFORMATION

Maps: OS maps are useful for locating crags, and essential when planning a mountain day. The 1in Tourist map to Ben Nevis & Glencoe also conveniently includes Ardgour, Glen Etive, and the relevant parts of the Southern Highlands. However, the following maps are required for a complete coverage of the region in 1:50,000 scale:

Arran   Sheet 69
Arrochar   Sheet 56
Southern Highlands & Glen Etive   Sheet 50

Ardgour   Sheet 40
Glencoe & Ben Nevis   Sheet 41
Creag Meaghaidh   Sheet 35

Comprehensive Guidebooks: The Scottish Mountaineering Club publishes a series of rock and ice guides, four of which, at the time of writing, cover most of the area under consideration here. For updating route descriptions, and for useful general information, the annual SMC Journal is highly recommended.

EMERGENCIES
First Aid Checklist

Check Breathing
- If necessary, clear the airway using a hooked finger to remove obstructions such as vomit, blood, and teeth.
- Turn the casualty to lie in the recovery position (unless you suspect spinal injury). This helps to maintain a clear airway.

Check For Severe Bleeding
- Apply direct pressure from a pad to stop bleeding.
- Elevate the limb.

Check For Broken Bones
- Do not move the casualty if a spinal injury is suspected.
- Immobilise other fractures using improvised splints and slings.

Monitor Condition
- Keep the casualty warm and comfortable while awaiting rescue (protect from wind and insulate from the gound).
- Reassure the casualty and monitor his condition regularly.

Alert Mountain Rescue
Dial 999, ask for police/mountain rescue, and try to have the following written details ready:
- Name and description of injured person.
- Precise position of the injured person on the crag.
- Location of the crag (including *grid reference* and *map sheet number*).
- Time and nature of accident.

- Extent of injuries.
- Indication of prevailing weather at the scene (cloud base, wind strength, visibility, etc.).
- Remain by the phone until met by a police officer or member of the rescue team.

Rescue Helicopters
- Secure all loose equipment before the helicopter arrives (weight rucksacks, jackets, etc. with stones).
- Identify yourself by raising your arms in a V as the helicopter approaches. Do *not* wave.
- Protect the injured person from rotor downdraught (which is intense).
- Allow the winchman to land of his own accord.
- Do not approach the helicopter unless directed to do so by one of the crew (danger from rotors, exhaust, etc.).

A FINAL CAUTIONARY NOTE

A guidebook of this sort reflects the author's own reactions and responses to the routes. Not everyone will agree on the exact lines to follow, the levels of difficulty encountered, or the best techniques to apply. When faced by an unexpected route-finding problem, you would be wise ultimately to trust your own intuition.

Possible author errors are not the only reason to stay alert; dramatic changes can take place on the rock itself. There is no reason to suppose that ledges will cease to erode, or buttresses collapse, in the intervening period between this book going to press and your reading of it. Winter climbs, obviously, vary enormously — not only year to year, but week to week.

If you *do* experience any difficulty because of an error on my part (for which I apologise, most sincerely, in advance), or because of changes to the crag itself, or indeed if you have any other comments on the guide, then please write to Ken Crocket, care of The Crowood Press. I would be very grateful, and your help in updating the guide will be acknowledged in future revisions.

Arran

The granite peaks of Arran rise proudly over the Firth of Clyde, only a few hours from Scotland's largest conurbation. But once having entered the rocky coires of the island's north-east corner, it is possible to experience a sense of remoteness and solitude normally encountered only in the most far-flung of mainland ranges.

A deep-formed granite is responsible for the interesting mixture of delicate and strenuous passages typical of Arran climbs. The coarse-grained rock is mostly sound (the gullies are an exception) and typically formed into huge, blocky walls. Areas of slabby rock often lure the visitor into attempting a harder climb than usual. Although the rock is rough, lichen renders it slippery in the wet, so large nuts and Friends are very useful (as is a thick skin!). With hindsight we can see that traditional tweed clothing had a lot going for it on the rough slabs and strenuous chimneys of Arran.

The best way to savour the island's charms (there is more to Arran than hills and rocks) is to take at least four days' holiday, although a weekend visit is perfectly feasible, if somewhat hurried. The best time to visit often proves to be on either side of summer. However, seasonal weather prediction is even more uncertain here than it is for other climbing areas.

Approaches: By car ferry from Ardrossan to Brodick (Sunday sailings in summer). It is probably not worth taking a car over. Buses circle the island from Brodick pier (useful for Glen Sannox).

Accommodation: Excellent campsites will be found in Glen Rosa and Glen Sannox. There is also a paying campsite in the lower stretches of Glen Rosa. Remote camping beyond the Garbh Allt is convenient for the climbing, but not for the facilities of Brodick; the very boggy path up Glen Rosa deters frequent trips in either direction. Rough howffs may be found under the Rosa Pinnacle. Cycle hire, shops, hotels, and other amenities are available in Brodick.

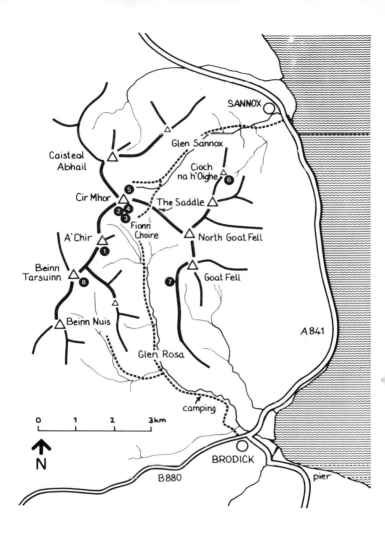

SANNOX

Glen Sannox

Caisteal
Abhail

Cioch
na h'Oighe
⑥

Cir Mhor
⑤
②④
③

The Saddle

Fionn
Choire

A`Chir
①

North Goat Fell

Beinn
Tarsuinn
⑧

⑦

Goat Fell

Beinn Nuis

A 841

Glen Rosa

camping

0   1   2   3km

N

BRODICK

pier

B 880

Descending on to the slabs during an early repeat of Sou'Wester Slabs (Route 4), Cir Mhor, Arran. (Photo: Ken Moneypenny)

The Triple Chimney finish, common to both Sou'Wester Slabs and South Ridge Direct (Route 3). (Photo: Ken Moneypenny)

1: A'CHIR RIDGE (M) 1600m +

Summary: One of the best ridge traverses in Scotland. Extensive views of the Firth of Clyde and the nearby Arran hills. The Gap and the *mauvais pas* provide most of the technical interest. Route-finding is not complicated and many variations can be found, including short problems of up to *VD* standard (the *M* grade assumes major difficulties will be avoided). Total distance 16km.

First Ascent: R.A. Robertson, J.H. Gibson, T.F.S. Campbell, Dr Leith and H. Fleming, January 1892.

Best Conditions: Spring and autumn are usually the best times, although given sufficient daylight the ridge may be traversed at any time of year (except when heavy snow conditions prevail).

Approach: From Brodick follow the Glen Rosa path to the bridge over the Garbh Allt (GR:982 387). Turn left on to the north bank of the burn and ascend the Cnoc Breac to the summit of Beinn a'Chliabhain. Now descend to the col between Coire a'Bhradain and Coire Daingean and follow the path rightwards below a rock face to gain the start of the ridge at GR:963 414. 3hrs.

Descent: From the col at the north end of the ridge (GR:968 429), descend easily into the Fionn Choire and follow the Glen Rosa path back to Brodick.

In 1892, J.H. Gibson and his party descended from the summit of A'Chir ('The Comb' — so named because of its serrated appearance), turned a step on its west side, and gained a gap where the ridge levelled out into a horizontal crest. Almost at once they came upon a *mauvais pas* (now marked by a cairn). A direct route would be impossible. They had to find another way. By descending a few metres down the east flank they gained an exposed, grassy ledge. It slanted downwards across the face and passed from sight. Trusting their instincts they followed the ledge to a rock trench which in turn brought them back on to the ridge at a small col. The *mauvais pas* was behind. The way ahead was now clear as they followed the ridge crest northwards towards Cir Mhor and the completion of what was to become one of Scotland's classic ridge traverses.

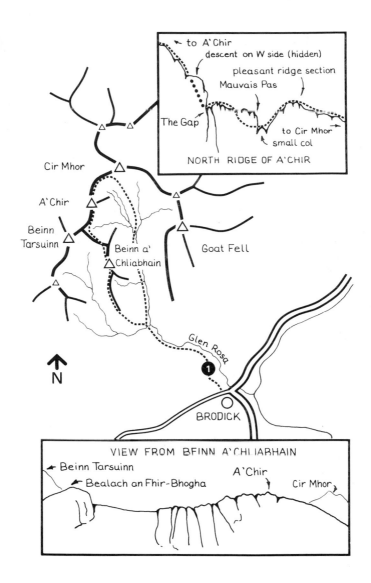

to A'Chir

descent on W side (hidden)

pleasant ridge section

Mauvais Pas

The Gap

to Cir Mhor
small col

NORTH RIDGE OF A'CHIR

Cir Mhor

A'Chir

Beinn
Tarsuinn

Beinn a'
Chliabhain

Goat Fell

Glen Rosa

1

N

BRODICK

VIEW FROM BEINN A'CHLIABHAIN

← Beinn Tarsuinn

← Bealach an Fhir-Bhogha

A'Chir

Cir Mhor

2: CALIBAN'S CREEP (D +) 150m

Summary: Varied and well-protected climbing, mainly following the exposed right edge of the ridge on rough, sound granite. The route continually surprises with its exposed and unusual situations. Excellent views of the neighbouring Rosa Pinnacle.

First Ascent: G.C. Curtis and G.H. Townend, July 1943.

Best Conditions: South facing. Generally dries out after a few hours of sunshine. Usually climbable from April to October.

Approach: Ferry from Ardrossan to Brodick then:
(1) Up Glen Rosa by a muddy footpath (refer to Arran area map), or (2) from Glen Sannox, gain the saddle between Goat Fell and Cir Mhor, descend a short way into Glen Rosa and finally contour into the Fionn Choire below Cir Mhor (GR:975 428). 3hrs.

Starting Point: Rosa Pinnacle dominates the scene, its west flank separated from the Caliban Ridge by Green Gully. Scramble up the gully's easy approaches to start at the toe of the buttress, at a square-cut overhang on its right side.

Descent: Down the open gully immediately west of the Caliban Ridge, followed by an eastward traverse below the ridge to regain the start.

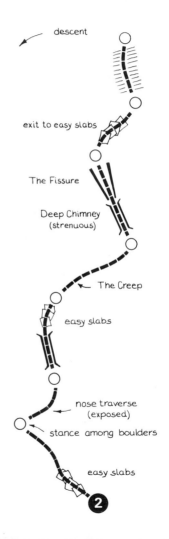

descent

exit to easy slabs

The Fissure

Deep Chimney
(strenuous)

The Creep

easy slabs

nose traverse
(exposed)

stance among boulders

easy slabs

2

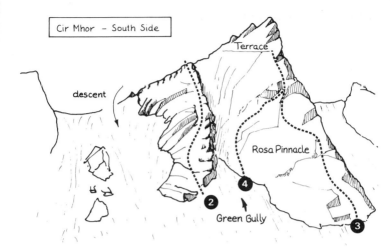

Cir Mhor – South Side

Terrace

descent

Rosa Pinnacle

④

②

→ Green Gully

③

Curtis and Townend were stationed during the war on the Firth of Clyde at Fairlie, within sight of the beautiful Isle of Arran, jewel of the Firth. Their explorations on Arran's superb granite peaks brought its climbing into the 20th century. Cir Mhor in particular – one of the island's finest peaks – became known as one of Scotland's outstanding mountains in terms of position, form and climbing.

Caliban's Creep begins innocently enough with an easy slab. The fun starts with a seemingly desperate traverse across an exposed wall, strangely reminiscent of Lake District climbing. This traverse (the holds are revealed to be good) takes one around the nose and into a typical Arran chimney – the first of several.

Beyond a slab the way ahead seems blocked by a vertical step in the ridge. Escape lies via the 'Creep', a stomach crawl through a tight hole on the right (those of generous girth may experience some difficulty!). The position is unusually exposed for the standard, but secure, and surely quite unique. Beyond it a traverse across the wall leads to another chimney with a strenuous move or two. The rock scenery is superb.

3: SOUTH RIDGE DIRECT (VS) 330m

Summary: Quite simply one of the best routes at this grade in the country.   Maintains   quality   of climbing and excellence of rock to the finish. In its entirety the route is long and entertaining, although the main difficulties are short and, on a sunny afternoon at least, not too serious. Three pitches warrant the *VS* grade: the S Crack, the Y Crack and the Layback.

First Ascent: J.F. Hamilton and D. Paterson, September 1941.

Best Conditions: South facing and therefore quick to dry during sunny weather. Most likely to be in condition from April to October.

Approach: As for Route 2, via Glen Rosa or Glen Sannox to the Fionn Choire below the cyclopean south ridge of Rosa Pinnacle.

Starting Point: Below disorganised slabs at the lowest point of the ridge, and directly below its vertical nose.

Descent: A large terrace separates upper and lower pinnacles. Traverse   this   leftwards   and descend beyond the Caliban ridge to reach an open gully (which is immediately west of the Caliban ridge). Descend the gully and then traverse east — passing below the Caliban ridge — to regain the starting point.

Two features split the otherwise impregnable nose of the South Ridge: the S Crack and the Y Crack. The elegant S Crack leads sinuously up to the belay ledge below overhangs (a pleasant surprise awaits you on this pitch). The wall above, broken by the Y Crack, is the crux. Fortunately the difficulties are short, if strenuous, and based on good holds within the cracks (unfortunate leaders have had their boots jammed here . .).

Beyond the crux an easy traverse leads across the top of the great western slabs to a sloping stance in a corner. Above rises the last hard pitch — the Layback. At the bulging slab most climbers will follow a line of holds leading out right to easier rock, whereas a strong leader will continue laybacking and follow Lovat up his strenuous variation.

After all this excitement the difficulty (though not the interest) diminishes as a three-tier chimney on the left of the crest leads to the ridge proper and the Terrace.

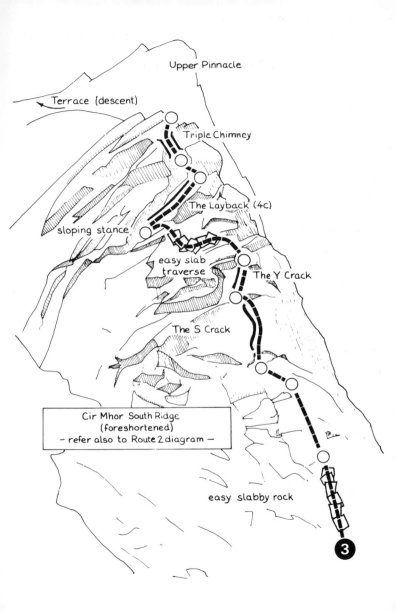

Upper Pinnacle

Terrace (descent)

Triple Chimney

The Layback (4c)

sloping stance

easy slab traverse

The Y Crack

The S Crack

Cir Mhor South Ridge
(foreshortened)
– refer also to Route 2 diagram –

easy slabby rock

3

4: SOU'WESTER SLABS (VD) 185m

Summary: Probably the best granite *V. Diff* in Scotland. The route follows a striking line of cracks and grooves up the vast slabs which flank the magnificent Rosa Pinnacle. The upper part, which is no less enjoyable, climbs the crest of the ridge as for Route 3. Purists will continue beyond the Terrace to climb the 75m Upper Pinnacle at *VD* standard.

First Ascent: G.H. Townend, G.C. Curtis, H. Hore and M.J.H. Hawkins, September 1944.

Best Conditions: As for Route 3

(dries quickly during sunny weather in the months April to October).

Approach. As for Route 2 (via Glen Rosa or Glen Sannox to Fionn Choire) then up the entrance to Green Gully). Scramble up grass to reach slabs of the west face of Rosa Pinnacle.

Starting Point: At a left-slanting groove (this is at the same level as the foot of the large vertical wall on the Caliban Ridge opposite).

Descent: As for Route 3.

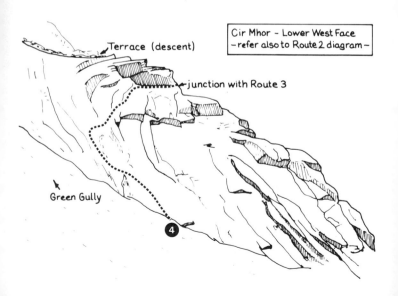

Terrace (descent)

junction with Route 3

Cir Mhor – Lower West Face
– refer also to Route 2 diagram –

Green Gully

④

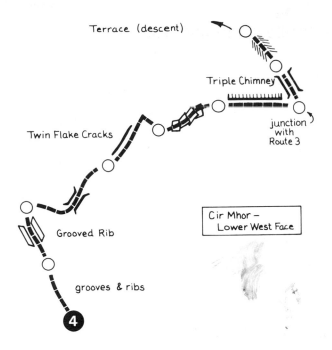

Terrace (descent)

Triple Chimney

junction
with
Route 3

Twin Flake Cracks

Grooved Rib

grooves & ribs

Cir Mhor –
Lower West Face

4

Sou'Wester Slabs is justifiably the most popular route on Arran. Its special appeal lies in climbing the improbable (and improbably rough) slabs by magnificent, parallel cracks.

The first two pitches follow left-trending grooves and ribs, until a short descending traverse leads easily right to an open chimney and spike belay below parallel cracks. By leaning out on comforting flake edges to maximise foot friction, these cracks are climbed to an exit at the right edge of the slab. The rock throughout is Arran granite at its superlative best. A few moves in rightward descent gain the lower slab which in turn leads to a belay below the huge overhang. Escape lies to the right: across to the edge to gain the foot of the Three-Tier Chimney of South Ridge Direct (Route 3).

5: POTHOLE SLAB (HVS) 115m

Summary: A modern line on an old face, taking sustained rock to an abrupt finish. Poorly-protected in places, with some route-finding difficulties.

First Ascent: J. Gillespie and W. Skidmore, June 1968.

Best Conditions: North-east facing and slow to dry. Allow at least three days of good weather.

Approach: Approach via Glen Sannox. Follow the north bank of the burn to where the path ascends to the saddle between Cir Mhor and Goat Fell. Now take a poor path which branches off to the right, following the south bank of the burn into Coire na h'Uaimh — the high coire below the triangular lower wall of the north-east face at GR:974 434. 2hrs.

Starting Point: C and D gullies breach the right-hand section of the lower wall, defining between them an area of slabs. This area is bounded on the left by a long and usually wet groove. Start in the centre of the main slab, below a pothole.

Descent: Descend a ledge carefully down to the right (looking in) into Gully D. Descend the gully (*M*) to regain the coire.

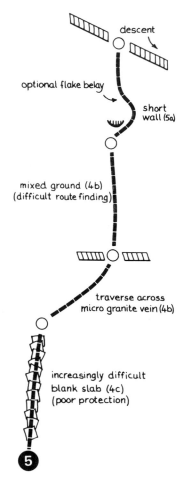

descent

optional flake belay

short wall (5a)

mixed ground (4b) (difficult route finding)

traverse across micro granite vein (4b)

increasingly difficult blank slab (4c) (poor protection)

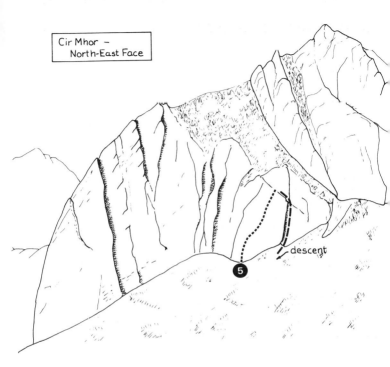

Loathsome gullies on the North-East Face occupied founder members of the SMC in the 1890s, but it was not until the 1960s that good rock routes began to appear. Pothole Slab, first climbed by members of the Greenock MC, was the best of them.

The first pitch climbs a fine slab above the curious pothole. Poor protection and increasing difficulty test the leader's confidence. A technically easy third pitch poses route-finding problems, although an experienced leader could climb it more or less directly and still stay out of trouble. Incidentally, the last pitch may be split by belaying on the good flake from where a leftward hand traverse gains the upper section.

6: TIDEMARK (S) 70m

Summary: Girdles the upper part of The Bastion, an impressive buttress high on the face. Includes steep slabs and a superb, natural gangway. Well worthwhile, despite a harrowing approach.

First Ascent: A.J. Maxfield, J. Peacock, June 1960.

Best conditions: Faces south-east but requires two or three days of good weather to dry out. Best months: April to October.

Approach: Via Glen Sannox. The 250m south-east face stands above the Devil's Punchbowl — Coire na Ciche — at GR:999 439. The ascent to it is both short and obvious. 1hr 30 mins.

Five parallel ledges, numbered 1 to 5 from bottom to top, slant across the face and all are loose and vegetated. Fortunately, Ledge 3 is the least unstable; follow it up to the right, passing under the magnificent vertical wall of The Bastion, to reach a stance on its right side.

Starting Point: At a spike belay above Ledge 3 (this position is some distance below and left from the termination of the ledge — refer to diagram).

Descent: The route finishes on Ledge 4. Follow this up to the right to the ridge, which can be descended to Ledge 3, and thence back down to the coire.

The enigmatic Maxfield seems to have recorded little else in Scotland other than his routes on Cioch na h'Oighe. Tidemark was a surprisingly good find here, and just reward for the nerve-racking approach scramble. Some years after this ascent, he drowned in an accident on an Aberdeenshire sea cliff.

The Bastion, that formidable buttress above Ledge 3, has the best rock on the mountain. Cunning and experience count for a lot during the approach, but once on the rock you will be able to enjoy the magnificent traverse across the upper part of the buttress.

Initially two delicate slabs lead to a split block situated a few metres along a curving gangway (there is an eye-hole belay anchor above). The gangway, which sweeps across The Bastion in glorious position, is the *raison d'être* for this whole enterprise and allows you to forget for a few minutes the effort and anguish of the approach.

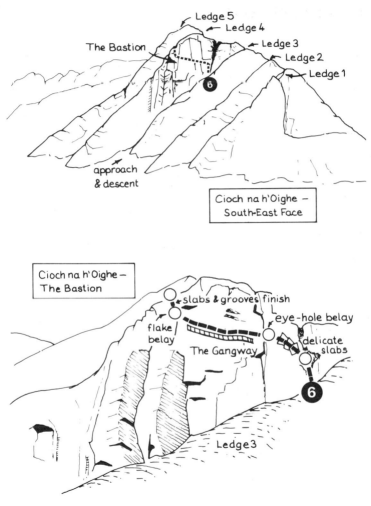

Ledge 5
Ledge 4
Ledge 3
Ledge 2
Ledge 1

The Bastion

⑥

approach
& descent

Cioch na h'Oighe –
South-East Face

Cioch na h'Oighe –
The Bastion

Slabs & grooves finish

eye-hole belay

flake
belay

The Gangway

delicate
slabs

⑥

Ledge 3

7: BLANK (S) 120m

Summary: The best route up a clean slab of rough granite. A good introduction to the harder routes hereabouts. Lack of protection makes for some exciting friction climbing.

First Ascent: B. Kennelly and A. McKeith, September 1963.

Best Conditions: Although the slabby exposure faces the afternoon sun, it requires a day or two to dry out after bad weather. Generally climbable in the months between April and October.

Approach: From Brodick follow the Glen Rosa path for about 2km beyond the bridge at GR:983 386 (at the junction of the Garbh Allt and the Rosa Water). The South Slabs will be seen high up on the right, about 300m above the path and to the right of the main slabs. (Note: if the river is high it may be better to cross by a small bridge about 200m above the junction with the Garbh Allt. This is not obvious from the path.) The crag is at GR:986 412. 2hrs 30mins.

Starting Point: Below the centre of the slab, about 3m right of a broken fault line which rises up to the left.

Descent: Traverse right from the top of the slab until beyond rock, and then scramble down heather to regain the foot.

Despite the long approach, Blank makes a good first route after a late arrival on the island (or as an evening alternative to the fleshpots of Brodick).

The smooth slab of the first pitch probably constitutes the crux. Unfortunately the nervous leader, having safely negotiated its perils, will find little solace in the poor stance above. Beyond this the confident will proceed by the line of their choice. The rock is excellent. Those less sure of themselves (or unable to take advantage of the latest generation of high-friction rock boots . . .) will contrive their line to take advantage of pock-holes in the granite. Either way, the lack of protection and poor belays will always lend a serious air to the climbing.

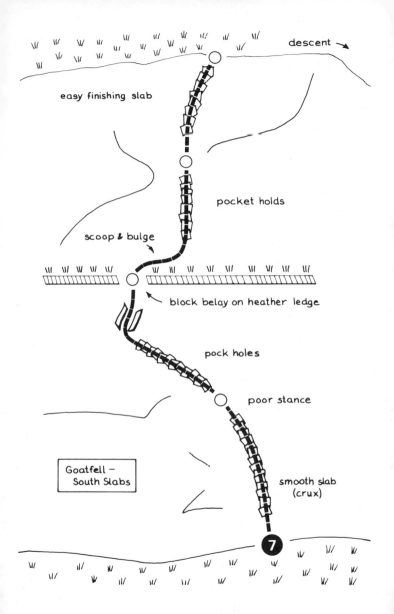

descent

easy finishing slab

pocket holds

scoop & bulge

block belay on heather ledge

pock holes

poor stance

Goatfell –
South Slabs

smooth slab
(crux)

7

8: THE BLINDER (E1) 135m

Summary: A striking and uncompromisingly modern line based on a major corner system. Includes plenty of well-protected jamming and bridging. Free moves over a roof on the second pitch constitute the crux.

First Ascent: J. Crawford and W. Skidmore, August 1971.

Best Conditions: South facing, but allow two or more fine days after wet weather. Generally climbable in the months between April and October.

Approach: From Brodick follow the Glen Rosa path to just before the bridge over the Garbh Allt at GR:983 386. Take the path which rises up the hillside (and later converges with the Garbh Allt) to enter Coire a'Bhradain. The Meadow Face will be seen to the left of the head of the coire at GR:961 412. 2hrs 30mins.

Starting Point: The route climbs a prominent corner up the south face of the buttress. Start below a steep corner crack just left of the pronounced left edge of the main face.

Descent: From the top of the crag, go left beyond a gully (Hanging Gully), before descending to regain the coire.

The ascent of this soaring corner with its roofs and bulges was one of 'Big' Bill Skidmore's best routes. Its classically direct line has immediate appeal.

On the first ascent the small roof on Pitch 2 demanded an aid nut, with another used above. But on later ascents, taking advantage of cleaner rock and a growing familiarity with the route, climbers were able to dispense not only with this aid, but also with the sling originally used to overcome the bulge on the third pitch.

Near the top of the route, while climbing up from the floor of a square recess, the pioneers were faced with the choice of two chimneys. Between them they had already accounted for four strenuous crack and chimney pitches, and the last thing they wanted now was a struggling exit from the face. The right-hand chimney looked easier, so they chose that. Some time later they discovered that the left-hand chimney had in fact been climbed already by Curtis and Townend's party in 1944 — as part of a *V.Diff*!

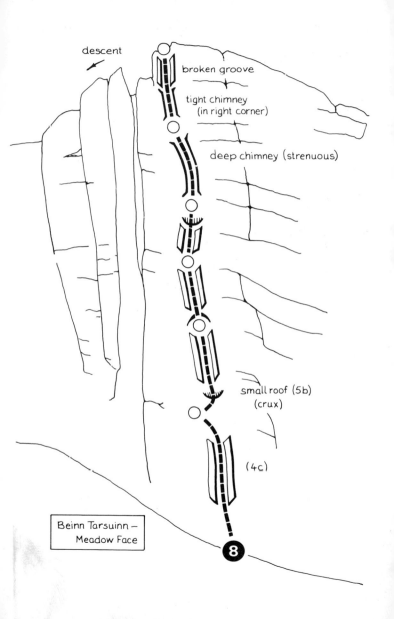

descent

broken groove

tight chimney
(in right corner)

deep chimney (strenuous)

small roof (5b)
(crux)

(4c)

Beinn Tarsuinn —
Meadow Face

8

Arrochar Area

On a good day, scores of walkers will make their way to Arrochar and its group of six principal hills known collectively as the Arrochar Alps. Although each hill has something to offer, most will climb the path leading to the Cobbler's three peaks.

The Cobbler, otherwise known as Ben Arthur, is a name often applied to the whole mountain, although strictly it refers only to the central summit, at 881m the highest of the three on the mountain. The other two are known as South Peak and North Peak. The resemblance of the summit block of Central Peak to a cobbler sitting at his work prompted the old local name of 'an greasaiche crom' — the crooked shoemaker. This block is sufficiently exposed and rocky to dissuade many non-climbers from attempting its ascent.

The Cobbler has long been a focal point for the best Scottish climbers. Interest kindled in the early days of the SMC was sustained through the 1930s by Jock Nimlin and friends, and into the post-war period of rising standards by members of the Creagh Dhu club. Several modern and very hard routes have been recorded during the 1980s.

It is easy to see why the Cobbler should have been responsible for so many advances in Scottish rock climbing. Access was very convenient from the urban sprawl of Scotland's central valley, with Arrochar just over an hour's drive from Glasgow. In earlier years, during the heyday of the Clyde steamer, Arrochar pier was a favourite stopping point from where superb views of the jagged mountain skyline were sure to tempt the adventurous.

It would be fair to say that the hill can boast the greatest concentration of good *Severe* climbs in Scotland. Its collection of excellent harder routes is a bonus. Most of the routes are short by Scottish standards, and few exceed 80m. In compensation, most of them have strong character, offering sustained climbing, interesting cruxes, and great situations.

The Cobbler is often at its best during April, May and early June. There are no restrictions on access. The rippling, schistose rock demands a confident balance technique and so tends to favour the stylish climber. It is best avoided if wet, when the ubiquitous lichen transforms it into the greasiest of rocks. Be careful with the tiny quartz holds which are brittle and liable to snap off. Medium-sized chockstones are particularly useful for protection.

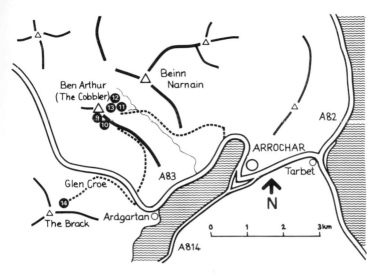

Approaches: The main centre is Arrochar, at the head of Loch Long (GR:298 046). From Glasgow, approach via the A82 Loch Lomond road (the Loch Long road from Helensburgh is narrow and twisting). By train, take the Glasgow-Oban-Fort William line from Glasgow Queen Street to Tarbet station. From Tarbet the pass road between Loch Lomond and Loch Long leads to Arrochar in 2km.

Accommodation: Hotels in Arrochar. Youth Hostel at Ardgartan (GR:273 030) on the west shore of Loch Long, 3km by road from Arrochar. East Kilbride MC hut (sleeps ten — apply to club secretary) in Glen Croe, about 1.5km west of Ardgartan. The hardy might use one of the several howffs situated high in the coire under the peaks of the Cobbler.

9: SOUTH-EAST RIDGE & ARETE (M) 200m

Summary: Exposed but easy climbing over two of the Cobbler's three peaks, leading satisfyingly to one of the few summits in Britain unattainable by walking.

First Ascent: South-East Ridge — G. Thomson and party, October 1889. The Arete — W.W. Naismith and G. Thomson, July 1894.

Best Conditions: April to October. Allow two days of dry, sunny weather. Some sections remain damp for longer because of grass ledges.

Approach: (1) From Arrochar. Approach as for Route 11, then cross the coire under the boulder field towards the South Peak at GR:260 057, or (2) from Glen Croe as for Route 10. 2hrs.

Starting Point: At the foot of the ridge.

Descent: Reverse the last few moves and descend to a ledge on the south side of the summit block. Now go along an exposed ledge to a window and so to easy ground. The traverse may be completed by walking across to the North Peak.

The South-East Ridge follows approximately the skyline as seen from the coire, but there is some scope for variation. At the first ledge either deviate to a chimney on the left, or continue more directly by an edge on the right. Above, the climbing will generally seem easier towards the left, and more exposed and difficult towards the right. The ridge leads to the small rocky summit.

The next objective is the grassy col between South Peak and Central Peak. The descent to it looks improbable. Start approximately above the middle of the North-West Face and descend a short wall in a corner. Now go down and right (all these directions apply when facing outwards) for a short distance, and then follow a grass ramp down and left to reach a grass ledge. This leads back right to the col.

The Arete leading to the Central Peak lies ahead. On the final section, a fine crack and traverse lead to the very summit — a uniquely isolated block pierced by two windows. Views from here include the nearby North Peak, with its overhanging beaks of rock, and the surrounding peaks and lochs of the Arrochar Alps.

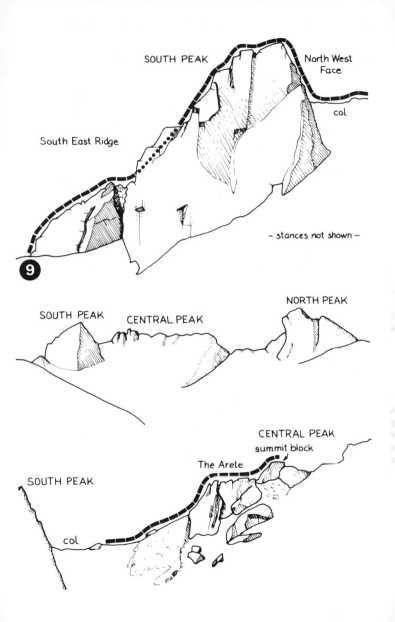

SOUTH PEAK

North West Face

col

South East Ridge

— stances not shown —

9

SOUTH PEAK

CENTRAL PEAK

NORTH PEAK

CENTRAL PEAK

summit block

The Arête

SOUTH PEAK

col

10: GLADIATOR'S GROOVE DIRECT (HVS) 70m

Summary: Follows a strenuous, zigzagging line to provide a good, varied introduction to the delights of this steep face. By the Direct Start it gives sustained climbing with surprisingly subtle difficulties.

First Ascent: W. Smith and H. MacInnes, August 1951. Direct Start — W. Smith and R. Hope, June 1952.

Best Conditions: Faces west and therefore dries quickly during the months April to October. In fine weather it receives the afternoon and evening sun (when it can become very hot).

Approach: (1) From Arrochar as for Route 11, then cross the coire under the boulder field to gain the South-East Ridge of the South Peak, the lower part of which gives access to the West Face, GR:260 057, or (2) from Glen Croe: start from the road north of the Youth Hostel and strike uphill alongside the forest to gain the South-East Ridge. 2hrs by either route.

Starting Point: An overhang terminates the right side of the West Face. Left of the overhang, a band of quartz crosses a smooth, vertical wall which is just right of a shallow, broken groove. Start below the quartz.

Descent: Go right and descend steeply by grass ledges on to the South-East Ridge.

The Direct gives strenuous climbing from the start, where a small overhang gives access to the quartz wall. It comes as a shock to be confronted at 20m with a delicate, rightward traverse. The wall is slabby here, but there are no handholds.

The climbing momentarily eases beyond the traverse and the terrace stance is soon gained. Ardgartan Arete (*S*), the right-bounding ridge of the face, is not far away.

A leftward diagonal rejoins the line of the original route; together they tackle a steep groove and an awkward corner before gaining a ledge below the final pitch. The easy finishing crack rises above. But beware: the leader who tries to mantel on to the sloping ledge below it will be in for a shock.

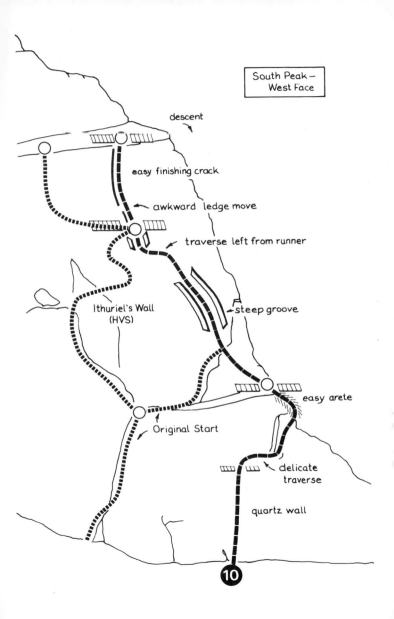

South Peak — West Face

descent

easy finishing crack

awkward ledge move

traverse left from runner

Ithuriel's Wall
(HVS)

steep groove

easy arete

Original Start

delicate
traverse

quartz wall

10

11: WETHER WALL/WHITHER WETHER (VS) 95m

Summary: Links two of the best mid-grade pitches on the Cobbler. The serious second pitch is set in a remarkably exposed position.

First Ascent: Wether Wall — J. Cunningham and H. MacInnes, September 1951. Whither Wether — H. MacInnes and W. Smith, August 1952.

Best Conditions: April to October. Allow two days of dry, sunny weather after rain (the first pitch may take longer to dry). Choose a calm day to attempt the delicate second pitch.

Approach: From Arrochar village go north along the road until a little way beyond the head of the loch. A lay-by on either side of the road marks the start of the path (GR:294 048). The path goes up through trees to join a ramp of concrete slabs. This in turn leads to a path which contours leftwards to a dam. Now follow the Buttermilk Burn, passing the Narnain Boulders. Cross the burn a little higher. The path is obvious and leads under the North Peak, passing the lowest rocks, to below the obvious Ramshead Gully. GR:260 059. 2hrs.

Starting Point: About 45m up Ramshead Gully, at the foot of a deep chimney. The route climbs the left wall of the gully.

Descent: Cross the summit then go down slabby rock to the west. Now go south to where the approach path gains the col between North and Central peaks.

This route brings together two wall pitches of contrasting character. The first, which takes a steep wall directly over a flake bulge, is technically the more difficult, whereas the second is far more exposed and serious — it provides an exhilarating lead up the buttress crest, and is arguably one of the best *Severe* pitches in the region. This is Cobbler climbing at its best, demanding total confidence from the leader.

The long second pitch begins above the shelf with difficult moves. Soon you will turn the right edge and encroach on to the main wall. Don't ignore the old bolt runner here before gaining the edge — little else follows! Stay close to the left edge of the main wall where feasible; the situations are impressive but the holds are better.

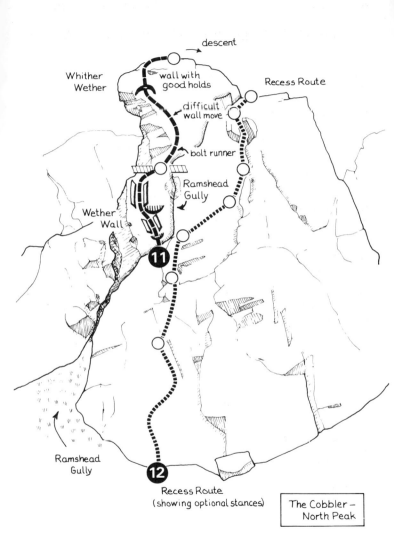

descent

Whither Wether

Recess Route

wall with good holds

difficult wall move

bolt runner

Ramshead Gully

Wether Wall

11

Ramshead Gully

12

Recess Route
(showing optional stances)

The Cobbler –
North Peak

12: RECESS ROUTE (VD) 110m

Summary: A strong line (one of the longest on the mountain) with classic chimneys, delicate wall moves, and an overhanging chockstone thrown in for good measure. Good situations abound.

First Ascent: J.B. Nimlin, J. Fox and R. Ewing, May 1935. (The crux pitch — The Fold — was first climbed by H. Raeburn and party, October 1904.)

Best Conditions: Being a mountain crag, the Cobbler is not generally suitable for rock climbing outside the April to October period. However, this particular route may be feasible after several sunny winter days, provided there is no snow melt. Note that the slightest amount of moisture on the mica schist rock renders it impossibly greasy.

Approach: From Arrochar village as for Route 11. Leave the path at the lowest rocks of the North Peak. 2hrs.

Starting Point: At the foot of a cracked slab, just left of an overhung recess at the lowest rocks.

Descent: Cross the summit, then go down slabby rock to the west. Now go south to where the approach path gains the col between North and Central peaks.

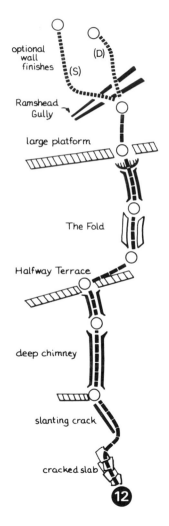

optional
wall
finishes   (S)   (D)

Ramshead
Gully

large platform

The Fold

Halfway Terrace

deep chimney

slanting crack

cracked slab

12

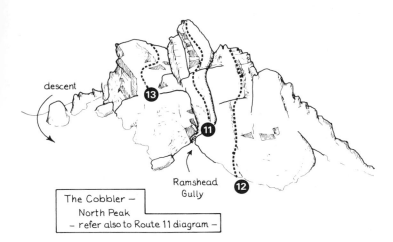

descent

13

11

Ramshead
Gully

12

The Cobbler —
North Peak
— refer also to Route 11 diagram —

Harold Raeburn visited the Cobbler on the last day of October 1896. With Willie Tough he traversed Halfway Terrace from Ramshead Gully, but declined to attempt the crux corner known as The Fold. They reversed their route down the gully. Raeburn, one of this country's most determined mountaineers, returned in 1904 with a large and merry party which included two ladies. Approaching by the same line, he succeeded in climbing The Fold, the hardest pitch on the route.

The first pitch links a series of polished, scalloped holds set among a slabby wall. It has an awkward move high up, protected by a small nut runner. The rest is obvious — a series of deeply incised corners rising up the crest of the buttress. The crux pitch, hopefully dry, gives several delightful moves on the left wall. The overhang above is thankfully secure.

The route ends below the final wall of the North Peak (taken by Whither Wether on its extreme left), but two optional 25m finishes await: by Ramshead Wall (*D*), directly up a quartz-studded wall at the top of Ramshead Gully; or by Telepathy Crack (*S*) which starts further left.

13: PUNSTER'S CRACK (S) 50m

Summary: A short but action-packed climb of three pitches, finishing up an improbable wall. The scalloped schist holds demand good balance technique. Fortunately this particular route is well-endowed with good holds.

First Ascent: J. Cunningham and W. Smith, August 1949.

Best Conditions: Rarely in condition outside the April to October period. The rock is mica schist and very dangerous when wet; allow at least two dry summer days after rain.

Approach: From Arrochar village as for Route 11. Continue along the obvious path which passes beneath the North Peak. Just before reaching the col between Central and North peaks, traverse right beneath the summit cliffs of North Peak to below the start of the climb. 2hrs.

Starting Point: Just left of a deep chimney slot, between the obvious large corner of Right-Angled Gully on the right, and an overhung recess on the left.

Descent: Cross the summit, then go down slabby rock to the west. Now go south to where the approach path gains the col.

The Cobbler and its demanding balance climbing has always been accessible to climbers from the Glasgow area. In particular these cliffs were developed by members of that city's famous mountaineering club, the Creagh Dhu. 'Long' John Cunningham, who became one of the most widely known of the Creagh Dhu, gave the Cobbler and Scotland one of its best *Severes* in Punster's Crack. The climb zigzags elegantly up the cliff, taking the only reasonable way around a spectacularly overhanging section.

Bill Smith, Cunningham's partner that day, was just as assured and able. Perhaps the second pitch, a traverse right over a bottomless groove, belonged to him. An excellent nut runner now protects the move across this groove (awkward for the tall, but do not descend into the groove itself).

The very fine last pitch takes the open wall to the top. A crack and other holds invisible from below now materialise to reassure the understandably nervous newcomer. Take care with the small quartz holds, which are liable to snap off. The rock is otherwise excellent.

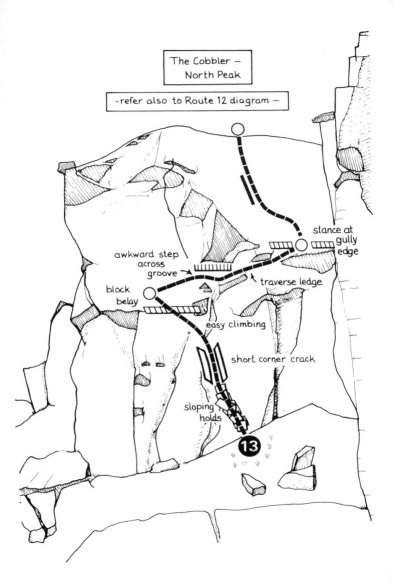

The Cobbler —
North Peak

-refer also to Route 12 diagram —

stance at
gully edge

awkward step
across
groove

traverse ledge

block
belay

easy climbing

short corner crack

sloping
holds

13

14: GREAT CENTRAL GROOVE (IV/V) 90m

Summary: A hard and sustained ice climb — one of the best in southern regions.

First Ascent: Original route — W. Skidmore and R.T. Richardson,. January 1968. Right-hand route — N. Muir and A. Paul, February 1977.

Best Conditions: Normally comes into condition during a prolonged freeze early in the winter, January and February being the best time (allow at least one week of sub-zero temperature). The iced-up slabs can be seen from the Rest-And-Be-Thankful road; if they appear black or grey then the route is not in condition.

Approach: Refer to the Arrochar map. Follow a forestry road on the south side of Glen Croe for about 2km until beyond a double bend. Leave the road where it bends to the right and crosses a burn. Follow a faint path on the east bank of the burn to open hillsides. The cliffs will be obvious above. 1hr 20 mins.

Starting Point: The route takes the obvious groove in the centre of the large, upper cliff. Start on a ledge to the left of the first corner.

Descent: Go west, skirting cliffs, to descend into the north-east coire. Cross the coire to regain the approach burn.

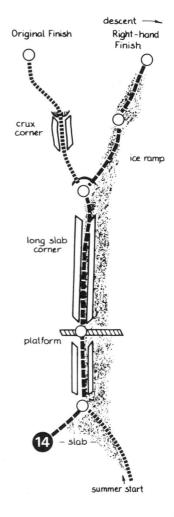

descent →
Original Finish   Right-hand
                        Finish

crux
corner

ice ramp

long slab
corner

platform

14 – slab –

summer start

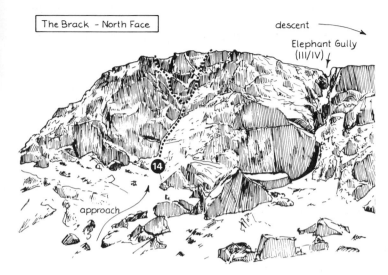

descent ──────→

Elephant Gully
(III/IV)

approach

14

Great Central Groove follows a satisfyingly median line on a cold north face. In good conditions, crampons will bite into waves of ice formed over slabs on the right wall, enabling the first steep chimney (a short one) to be overcome.

Above a large platform (and optional belay) the groove leads into a long slab corner. You may find a peg at its foot, and a thin crack in the corner itself. These help protect a sustained lead on which overlaps prove to be the most difficult obstacles. Finally you will pass a block on the right to gain a recess belay at the fork.

The original route, which was climbed in nails by those who made the first ascent, goes up steep corners and over an overhang. In the thinly-iced conditions normally found here, the overhang may succumb only to some desperate thrashing in aid slings. Alternatively, you might follow Norrie's Finish up its obvious rightward ramp. In good conditions this will be draped in masses of ice, warranting a grade of *IV*. This right hand route is probably the better finish for modern, front-pointing ice climbers.

Southern Highlands

Winter climbing in the Southern Highlands has always had its followers, mostly among local climbers who appreciate quiet days spent on the frozen turf and ice-smeared rocks of relatively obscure hills. The fact that some climbs in the region are technically very hard, and of up to 200m in length, clearly invalidates past criticisms that routes here are short and easy.

Winter climbing in the Southern Highlands takes place on crags of metamorphic rock (usually schist), which tends to be vegetated. Frozen turf and moss can be of material assistance on many of these routes. Treat these substances as you would perfect snow ice; they will hold picks and drive-ins with the utmost security.

Approaches: With the exception of Great Central Groove (Route 14), which has been included with the Arrochar routes, winter climbs of the Southern Highlands are approached either from Tyndrum (for Ben Lui) or Bridge of Orchy (for Beinn an Dothaidh and Beinn Udlaidh). Both are situated on the A82 between Glasgow and Glencoe, and both are served by rail. It may be convenient to climb on the Bridge of Orchy hills from a base in Glencoe itself, which is less than 30mins away by road. Stob Ghabhar also appears under this heading, although strictly speaking it belongs to the Central Highlands. Refer to individual route headings for approach details.

Accommodation: The combination of camping and Scottish winter climbing cannot be recommended. Often the only alternative is to book into a climbing hut or stay at a hotel.

Climbs around Bridge of Orchy have the hotel and station as focal points. The West Highland Way crosses the A82 here, and some wild camping may be found near the River Orchy. The Scottish Ski Club have a comfortable hut at Inverveigh (GR:293 389), 1km south-west of Bridge of Orchy. Amenities are also being developed at Tyndrum. The restrictive hotel hours of past years are now over, and most will be open throughout the winter.

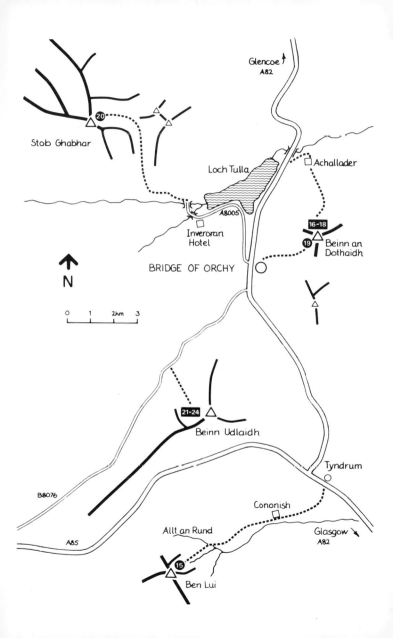

15: CENTRAL GULLY (I) 180m

Summary: Ascends the classic-ally formed peak of Ben Lui, which is sparingly glimpsed from the A82. The gully normally provides an uncomplicated ascent on snow, with a choice of finishes on to the summit ridge. In loose snow conditions, however, the rib to its left (South Rib, grade *I/II*) may offer a safer alternative.

First Ascent: A.E. Maylard, W. Brunskill, W. Douglas and J. Maclay, December 1892 (descended by W.W. Naismith, W.R. Lester and T.F.S. Campbell, April 1891).

Best Conditions: The amount of snow cover will be apparent from the road; there will be sufficient for an ascent if the steep, upper part of the north-east coire is covered. Freezing conditions are preferable to lessen the risk of avalanche.

Approach: The most scenic approach is by the Cononish Glen, starting from Tyndrum Lower Station. Follow a private road leading to Cononish Farm, and then a forestry road to the Allt an Rund (just past the farm, on the right, is the Eas Anie — a foaming waterfall in summer but an interesting grade *III/IV* climb after a good winter freeze). Cross the burn and continue more steeply by a faint path on the north-west flank of the burn which issues from the north-east coire. 2hrs.

Starting Point: From the floor of Coire Gaothaich, below the north-east face of Ben Lui (GR:270 266).

Descent: From the summit, go along to the North Top and descend the north-north-east ridge (Stob Garbh) until an easy descent can be made into the Coire Gaothaich.

The building of the railway to the north in the last decade of the nineteenth century opened up many mountain areas in Scotland. In particular it made a tourist centre out of the previously sleepy village of Tyndrum. The SMC were quick to take advantage. At the end of 1892, some of the great names gathered for a New Year Meet at Tyndrum. On the last day of the year they staged a mass attack on Ben Lui. Four climbers made a head-on approach up the centre of the coire. It was bitterly cold and icy as the pioneers kicked their way up easy slopes to gain the first of the rocky ribs that descend from the North-East Ridge. In the mist they moved slightly left to enter and climb what they guessed, correctly, would be the gully leading to the summit.

The gully is fairly well defined for about 100m, then opens up somewhat below the final slopes. If the summit ridge is corniced, a detour may have to be made to one side. Otherwise follow the pioneers and trend slightly left, emerging below the large summit cairn.

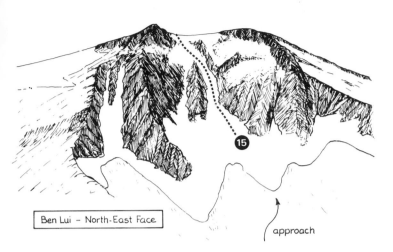

Ben Lui – North-East Face

approach

On a clear day you will be rewarded by a superb view over the Southern Highlands — the Paps of Jura, Ben More on Mull, Ben Cruachan, the Blackmount Hills, and of the Glencoe and Ben Nevis giants to the west and north. To the east, the hills of the Bridge of Orchy group dominate, while further south may be seen Ben Lawers, Ben More and Stobinian, and the Loch Lomond mountains.

Ben Lui is thought by many to be one of the most splendid mountains in the Southern Highlands, and rightly so. Its classic shape, height and position are well matched by the interest of its north-east coire. The routes may not be technically hard, but they will satisfy.

16: TAXUS (III/IV) 240m

Summary: A secluded snow and
ice gully of the traditional type,
leading to the top of the mountain.
An ice pitch at its foot usually
constitutes the crux, although a
harder variation finish may be taken
if desired.

First Ascent: Original route –
A.W. Ewing and A.J. Trees, March
1969. Ice-fall Finish – J. Crawford,
W. Skidmore, D. Dawson and J.
Madden, January 1976.

Best Conditions: A fairly good
cover of snow on the hills is
required, but the route should then
remain in condition for some time.
The key to success will usually be
the first pitch.

Approach: Follow the A82 north
from Bridge of Orchy for about 5km.
From the north-east end of Loch
Tulla (GR:321 443), follow a track
towards Achallader Farm (park just
before reaching the farm). A path
leads south from the farm to cross
the railway by a footbridge.
Continue over rough, undulating
ground, following the west bank of
the Allt Coire Achaladair. Turn up to
the right to enter the north-east
coire below the cliffs. These cliffs
are mostly hidden from the main
road by a northern spur of the hill,
but can be seen from the farm. 1hr
30 mins.

Starting Point: About one-third
of the way up the left flank of West
Gully (refer to diagram).

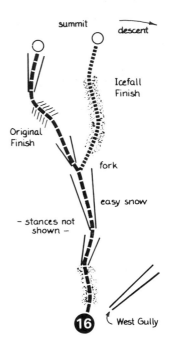

Descent: Follow the tilting
plateau east from the summit to the
col between Beinn an Dothaidh and
Beinn Achaladair. Descend easily
to regain the approach path by the
Allt Coire Achaladair.

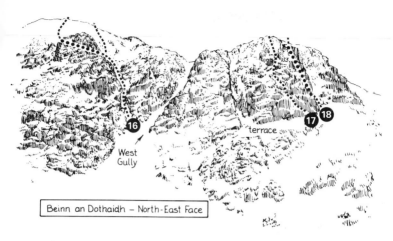

Beinn an Dothaidh – North-East Face

Amazingly, the line of Taxus was first attempted in 1894, by a party of SMC members staying at the Inveroran Inn. They had noticed it while engaged on the first ascent of West Gully the previous day. In the event they found the gully full of ice and decided that it would probably be too severe a tax upon their time. The route was left slumbering in this quiet coire for a further 75 years, until eventually it was climbed and named Taxus — probably as a word-play on the original reference.

The state of the first pitch can decide the outcome; it may be too icy, or even absent. Once overcome, however, the remainder of the gully should be straightforward as far as the upper fork below a summit buttress. From here the easy left fork leads to a snow ridge, followed to an easy left traverse into a narrow gully. This in turn leads to the summit plateau. As a harder alternative, and given sufficient build-up of ice, the Ice-fall Finish may be taken. It climbs the steep buttress above the fork in two or three pitches, emerging at the actual summit.

17: WEST BUTTRESS (III) 120m

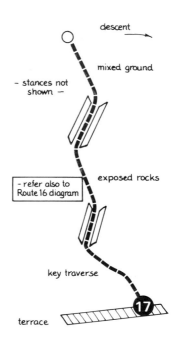

Summary: An entertaining and fairly sustained mixed route up the impressive main buttress.

First Ascent: J. Crawford, D. Dawson and W. Skidmore, February 1976.

Best Conditions: A light snow cover followed by a freeze should bring the route into condition. Much of the climbing relies on frozen turf. Conditions can vary quickly, although January and February should be the most reliable.

Approach: As for Route 16 to enter the north-east coire. Go up to the right, below the lowest rocks of the face, until an easy ledge leads back left under the main cliff.

Starting Point: Where a broad, tapering shelf runs out leftwards above the undercut base of the buttress (refer to diagram).

Descent: As for Route 18.

This route is a good example of Southern Highlands buttress climbing, in that the condition of the snow is almost irrelevant. Instead, while traversing out over the undercut base of the buttress on the first pitch, one worries about the state of the vegetation: will the turf be frozen? Is there enough of it? Can the drive-in be recovered from its firm placement? This traverse is the key to the whole route in that it gains the central system of chimney-grooves. Once established here, success on the remainder of this gradually reclining face is assured.

18: CIRRUS (III/IV) 140m

Summary: A strong and sustained chimney-gully line. The crucial ice pitch exceeds 80 degrees. Simple route-finding!

First Ascent: J. Crawford, J. Gillespie and W. Skidmore, March 1974.

Best Conditions: The quality of the snow is important for this route. Too much loose snow would render it very difficult, if not impossible. February or March might be the best months.

Approach: As for Route 17.

Starting Point: At the foot of the obvious deep chimney (refer to diagram).

Descent: Continue to the summit, or go west, skirting the top of the cliff, and descend in a rightward curving line to reach the top of the coire. Easy snow slopes then lead down into the coire below the cliffs.

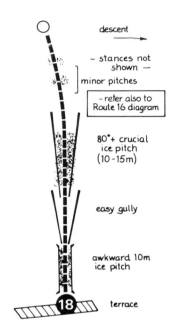

descent

– stances not shown –

minor pitches

- refer also to Route 16 diagram

80°+ crucial ice pitch (10 - 15m)

easy gully

awkward 10m ice pitch

18 terrace

Cirrus, along with many other quality routes of the Southern Highlands, was first climbed by members of Greenock MC, under the unofficial leadership of 'Big' Bill Skidmore. Activity on this cliff reached its zenith in the mid-1970s. Despite some Glaswegian rivalry, Skidmore's team accounted for the best lines on the buttress, Cirrus included.

Normally the narrow lower section of the climb leads to an ice pitch at about half-height. This is the crux, and it may involve about 10 – 15m of steep ice climbing before relenting. If conditions are good there may be two more ice pitches above, though neither will be as difficult as the main one.

19: SALAMANDER GULLY (III/IV) 150m

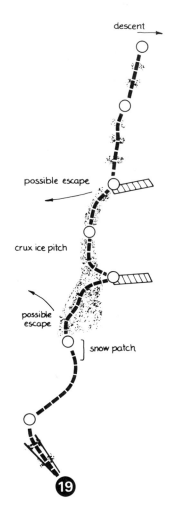

descent

possible escape

crux ice pitch

possible escape

snow patch

19

Summary: A surprisingly varied and enjoyable gully, leading to a spectacular ice-fall. Difficulties vary according to whether the ice-fall is climbed directly, indirectly, or avoided altogether.

First Ascent: K.V. Crocket and J.A.P. Hutchinson, January 1976.

Best Conditions: Normally comes into condition after a good freeze and with a little snow. Faces west in a sheltered coire; avoid on sunny days.

Approach: From Bridge of Orchy on the A82. Follow the uphill road opposite the hotel and park at the station. Go under the railway line and follow a path alongside the south bank of the Allt Coire an Dothaidh. Above the point where a tributary joins from the north, head up and slightly left to arrive at the left side of the cliff which dominates the coire. GR:324 403. 1hr 20 mins.

Starting Point: Near the left end of the cliff, below a shallow gully (refer to diagram).

Descent: Descend the ridge southwards to gain the col between Beinn an Dothaidh and Beinn Dorain. From here an easy descent leads back into the coire to regain the approach.

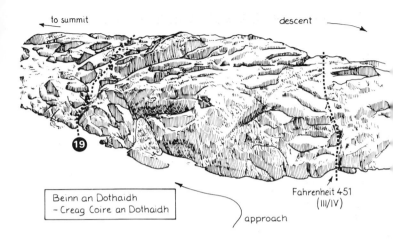

to summit

descent

⑲

Beinn an Dothaidh
– Creag Coire an Dothaidh

Fahrenheit 451
(III/IV)

approach

The name given to the coire by the Highlanders translates as 'the coire of the scorching', which is never more appropriate than during calm, sunny days when the coire transforms itself into an efficient sun-trap. These are not ideal conditions for ice climbing and it might be best to wait for a cold, overcast day. The route name, incidentally, continues this theme and refers to the animal in folklore which lives in fire.

Salamander is a deceptive route, the delights of its main ice-fall remaining hidden until close at hand. The prospect of interesting climbing and good scenery encourages investigation by the curious climber.

Initial easy pitches in a winding gully lead pleasantly to a two-pitch ice-fall which is the pride of the route. The fall has two distinct sections, broken by a ledge. The lower section, set at a reasonably gentle angle, can be climbed almost anywhere but is easiest on the left. By contrast the upper section is very steep (80 – 90 degrees) and is climbed by trending up to the left over several bulges. Easier climbing beyond leads rightwards to the finish.

20: THE UPPER COULOIR (II) 90m

Summary: A long approach march through beautiful country, culminating in the ascent of a magnificent mountain · by its summit gully. Usually includes one pitch of 6 – 10m on 70 degree ice. A grand mountaineering day.

First Ascent: A.E. Maylard, Professor and Mrs Adamson, Miss Weiss, May 1897.

Best Conditions: The couloir holds snow throughout much of a typical winter. An ascent later in the season would be preferable, as by then the days will be longer and the snow more likely to be firm.

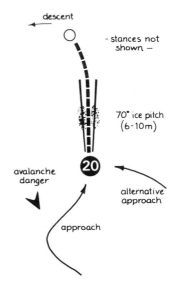

Approach: Leave the A82 at Bridge of Orchy and follow the A8005, around Loch Tulla, to Victoria Bridge (parking just past the bridge at GR:272 422). Take the footpath west from Forest Lodge, along the Linne nam Beathach, as far as Clashgour, the corrugated metal hut belonging to Glasgow University MC (as distinct from the farm at Clashgour further west). At the hut, turn uphill to follow the track north along the Allt Toaig. This leads to the col between Stob Ghabhar and Stob a'Choire Odhair (this is about 5km from Forest Lodge). Now contour west over rough ground, rising gently to enter the small north-east coire of Stob Ghabhar. GR:231 456. 2hrs 30mins.

Starting Point: Avoid a lower tier of easy rock on the left, then ascend rightwards to reach the upper part of the face. Start at the foot of the obvious gully splitting the summit buttress.

Descent: From the summit, descend the South-East Ridge to easy ground west of the Allt Toaig. Cross this to regain the approach track.

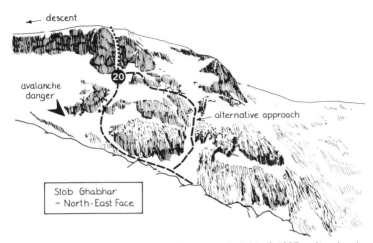

← descent

avalanche danger

20

alternative approach

Stob Ghabhar
– North-East Face

Stob Ghabhar (peak of the goat) rises to a height of 1087m. Its classic shape, reminiscent of Ben Lui, is well seen from several points on the A82 during the journey north. The Upper Couloir itself can be seen from Loch Ba on the Rannoch Moor, some distance beyond Bridge of Orchy.

The outing is a classic one in several respects: the approach walk is scenic, the climbing is elegant (but not too difficult), and the route finishes on the summit, the views from which are stunning.

Much of the pleasure derives from the approach. Its contouring line into the coire rewards with a wild and remote atmosphere. But take care: the final section has been known to avalanche. Assess conditions carefully before embarking on the final traverse towards the route.

The climb itself was the scene of several attempts during the last decade of the nineteenth century. One notable 'failure' in 1892 involved avoiding the crucial ice pitch by a difficult variation on the rocky rib to its right. As a consequence, the climbers were judged not to have completed a proper route!

21: QUARTZVEIN SCOOP (III/IV) 90m

Summary: An imposing route, climbed mainly on water-ice angled at up to 80 degrees and beyond. The crucial middle pitch climbs an ice-filled corner in a series of steep swoops, giving little respite.

First Ascent: T. Shepherd, T. Gray and D. Evans, 1979.

Best Conditions: The flat top of Beinn Udlaidh, and the horizontal strata of its metamorphic rocks, produce a constant weep of water over the lip of the north-facing coire. Consequently, many of the routes require only a freeze of several days duration to bring them into condition. The disadvantage is that water may be present on the routes despite sub-zero temperatures. Conditions are most likely to be favourable early in the season (late December and January). Later in the season, you may need to start early to minimise the risk from falling ice induced by extra sunshine, particularly on the left-hand side of the coire.

Approach: Leave the A82 when 1km south of Bridge of Orchy, and follow the B8074, down Glen Orchy, for 6km. Park at one of several small lay-bys just east of the confluence of the Allt Daimh and the River Orchy. The cliff is visible above. Cross a fence and field and find a way up the tortuous banks of the Allt Daimh into the coire. The slopes are under the scourge of forestry plantation, and

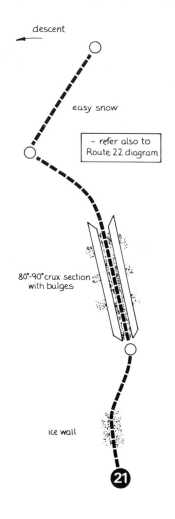

descent

easy snow

— refer also to Route 22 diagram

80°-90° crux section with bulges

ice wall

21

the best way will be found near the burn. The diagonal orientation of drainage ditches higher up the slope makes for very irritating walking.

The gently curving line of crags in Coire Daimh ('Coire of the Stags') is broken by several gullies. The Central Buttress is flanked to left and right by two obvious gullies — Central, sloping up to the left, and West, sloping up to the right and partly hidden from below. The stretch of cliff left of Central Gully culminates in Black Wall, which is often draped by impressive ice-falls, the most obvious being the funnel-shaped Captain Hook. GR:274 330. 1hr.

Starting Point: Below the left-hand end of the Black Wall, below a corner.

Descent: Go left along the rim of the coire, taking care not to slide down any of the icy scoops which abound here. Descend by the ridge to the north until easy slopes lead southwards back down into the coire.

Beinn Udlaidh translates as the 'dull or gloomy hill', and certainly in summer the coire is a truly dark and dripping place. However, winter transforms the summit springs into glistening white ice-falls, and after a week's solid freeze one can be guaranteed a good climb.

The first pitch reactivates muscle and nerve frozen while gearing-up in the dark shade of Coire Daimh. Easier ground above its short wall of ice leads to the foot of the big corner. The corner rises steeply above the belay, and there is little choice of route. A wise second will belay a little to the right, thus avoiding the lumps of water-ice prised off by the leader's picks. After the travails of the corner, an easy pitch leads effortlessly out on to the plateau which, with a bit of luck, will be bathed in bright sunshine.

22: CAPTAIN HOOK (V) 75m

Summary: A fine ice climb in the modern idiom, requiring both strength and nerve. A bulging ice-fall above the ramp normally provides the crux pitch.

First Ascent: C. Calow and D. Cuthbertson, February 1980.

Best Conditions: Refer to Route 21. It should be obvious from below whether or not the route is in condition. Avoid periods of strong sunshine late in the season.

Approach: As for Route 21 to the Black Wall on the left-hand section of the cliff.

Starting Point: Near the left of the Black Wall, a ramp slopes up to the right, starting from a point just right of the corner of Route 21. Captain Hook climbs the obvious, funnel-shaped ice-fall rising above the end of the ramp. Start directly below the ice-fall.

Descent: As for Route 21 (left along rim; down ridge to north; south down easy slopes back into coire).

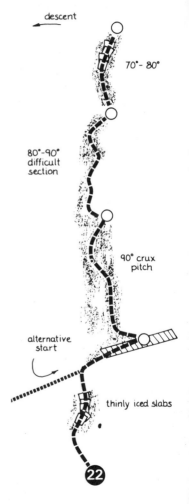

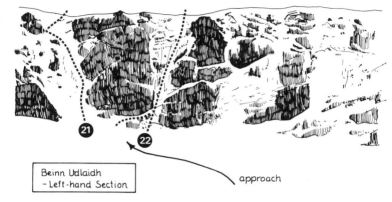

descent

- refer also to
Route 23 diagram -

Beinn Udlaidh
- Left-hand Section

approach

There is a school of thought that believes all ice routes to be the same. This is clearly false, as anyone who climbs in winter, and who has an average appreciation of natural phenomena, will tell you. There is no exhausting the variety of form. Ice is a natural wonder.

From a distance, the Captain Hook ice-fall appears to have a distinct shape. But closer inspection reveals the pillar to be less monolithic than it seemed; a decision will have to made as to the precise line to follow. Generally, the best line will ascend from bottom left to top right (although this need not preclude short diversions on the way). As the route will be different each winter, not to say each weekend, more explicit directions would be nonsensical.

A tired leader may decide to split the central pitch, despite the risk of invoking the second's displeasure. From this you will deduce (correctly) that the route is a good deal steeper than first appearances suggest!

23: WEST GULLY (II/III) 180m

Summary: A very pleasant and scenic gully up the right-hand side of Central Buttress. Normally contains two short pitches, and finishes with an interesting, easy-angled groove.

First Ascent: Not known.

Best Conditions: Unlike the buttress routes here, West Gully relies on snowfall to bring it into climbable condition. If snow lies on the coire floor, then there is a reasonable chance that the gully will contain sufficient material for an ascent.

Approach: As for Route 21. The wedge-shaped buttress in the centre of the coire is Central Buttress. It is flanked on either side by slanting gullies: Central Gully on the left and West Gully on the right. West Gully is not clearly seen from the approach, as it lies hidden behind Horny Ridge (a useful grade *I* escape route, should conditions in the gully be found to be dangerous).

Starting Point: At the foot of the gully, just right of the lowest rocks of Central Buttress.

Descent: Skirt above the cliffs to reach easy ground at their west end, and hence return to the coire floor (stay clear of the cliff edge in icy or misty conditions).

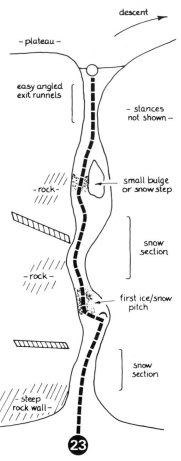

descent

– plateau –

easy angled exit runnels

– stances not shown –

– rock –

small bulge or snow step

snow section

– rock –

first ice/snow pitch

snow section

– steep rock wall –

23

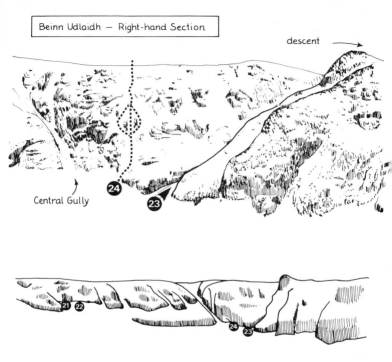

At a length approaching 200m, West Gully is a surprising find for this small coire. A steep wall of dark schist at the foot of Central Buttress marks the start. Uncomplicated snow leads to the first obstacle — a short ice or snow pitch. Below this, on the right, lean conditions may expose a tiny cave, although only a desperate climber would use it for shelter. The pitch leads up to the right, where more snow brings one to the second bulge in the gully. This is slightly steeper than the first, although perhaps not as high. Once over this, easy climbing leads to a gently-angled corridor which in turn leads out on to the plateau.

24: DOCTOR'S DILEMMA (IV) 180m

Summary: An interesting route, being a hybrid of both buttress and ice climbs. It ascends the Central Buttress by a series of short ice-falls, traverses, and easier mixed climbing. There is scope for variation in line, particularly in the middle section.

First Ascent: I. Duckworth and M. Firth, 1978.

Best Conditions: As for Route 21.

Approach: As for Route 21.

Starting Point: Just left of the lowest rocks of Central Buttress.

Descent: It might be possible to descend via Central Gully if conditions and visibility allow. However, the gully may contain a pitch, in which case it would be best to traverse rightwards across the top of the cliffs to reach easy ground. Descend over this to return to the coire floor.

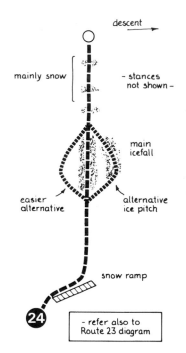

A snow ramp starts from a little way up to the left of the lowest rocks and leads easily back right. This ramp gives access to the buttress proper. Now look for an ice-fall below half-height, and zigzag up towards it. The faint-hearted will avoid the fall on the left, while in good conditions the bold will attempt a direct ascent. This section is probably the hardest on the buttress. Thereafter, steep snow interspersed with a few short ice steps leads to the top.

Glencoe Area

Glencoe is renowned for its bloody history and wild, impressive scenery. There are thirteen tops on the south side alone, while to the north is the best ridge scramble on the mainland — the Aonach Eagach. Glencoe also has the richest concentration of rock climbs in the country.

During wet and windy weather, the atmsophere in the glen can be oppressive. The lowered sky restricts the view to dark flanks of hills whose tops have been lost to the clouds; slopes of grey are relieved only by the white streaks of foaming burns. During the bright days of summer, it is altogether a different place — the hills are flecked with rock walls dried to a burnt umber or a light shade of grey, and great days among walls, corners, and grooves of rough rhyolite are promised.

The classically shaped Buachaille Etive Mor (highest top Stob Dearg, 1022m) will satisfy even the most discerning climber. This huge complex of buttresses, faces and gullies has routes of all grades, catering for every taste. Rock quality is for the most part superb, displaying excellent friction and a sometimes bewildering array of holds.

It would take several long holidays to explore the potential for rock climbing in the Bidean massif. There is even a choice of rock between the predominant rhyolite, and the grooved andesite of Stob Coire nan Lochan. Some routes here are easy of access, particularly those on the East Face of Aonach Dubh. These friendly rocks contrast with the higher and seemingly more serious crags such as E Buttress on the West Face of Aonach Dubh.

Though many of the steep walls found in Glencoe do not readily lend themselves to winter climbs, the area's many gullies and similar fault lines give some of the best winter routes in Scotland, including many classic lines. Vegetation is rarely present, most climbs relying on snow, ice, and snow-covered rock holds. Protection is infinitely better than that found further north on Ben Nevis. The most reliable conditions will be found on Stob Coire nan Lochan, thanks to its altitude.

The Trilleachan Slabs, set above the head of Loch Etive, complement the climbing found in Glencoe. The approach drive through the superb mountain scenery of Glen Etive, culminating with an alluring view down Loch Etive to Beinn Cruachan, is a joy in itself. The huge granite slabs are unique in this country, pitched at the precise angle for discomfiture yet thin possibility. Hopefully the latest developments in high-friction footwear will not make the climbing here too easy!

Approaches: The Glencoe hills are usually approached from the south, taking the A82 over the Rannoch Moor. Occupying the angle between Glencoe and Glen Etive is the Buachaille — the first mountain of interest to rock climbers to be seen when approaching from this direction. The road down Glen Etive branches off here, while the A82 steadily descends into Glencoe itself.

Glencoe is not served directly by rail. The nearest stations are Bridge of Orchy to the south, and Fort William to the north. The bus route between Glasgow and Fort William runs through Glencoe, but there is no service down the Glen Etive road (a narrow lane with passing places which ends at the head of Loch Etive). Much of Glencoe was purchased by Scottish climbing clubs and given to the National Trust for Scotland, thereby securing unrestricted access. An information centre is open from Easter to late autumn in Glencoe (GR:126 564).

Accommodation: Hotels popular among climbers include those at opposite ends of the glen: the Kingshouse Hotel (east), and the Clachaig Inn (west). Both also offer bunkhouse accommodation. Three climbers' huts may be booked through clubs: Blackrock Cottage (LSCC), just off the White Coires ski road at GR:267 531; Lagangarbh Cottage (SMC), opposite Altnafeadh at GR:222 559; and the Grampian Club Hut in Glen Etive at Inbhirfhaolin (GR:158 507). There are also several B&B houses in and around Glencoe village itself. Campsites are numerous, varying from wild pitches to commercial sites with facilities. The nearest shop selling climbing equipment will be found on the A828, a few hundred metres west of the Glencoe cross-roads.

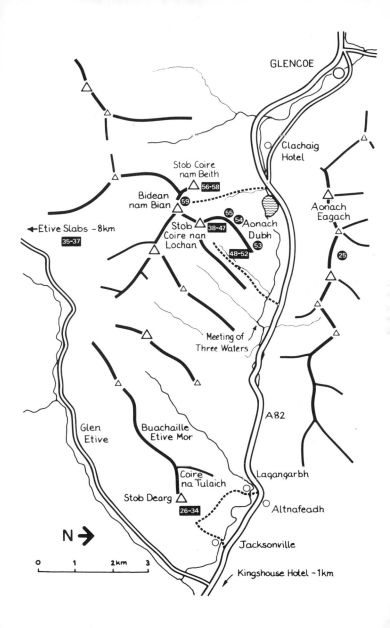

Spartan Slab (Route 35), Beinn Trilleachan, Glen Etive. (Photo: Ken Crocket)

Stuart Smith on Quiver Rib (Route 49), East Face of Aonach Dubh, Glencoe. (Photo: Ken Crocket)

Colin Stead on SC Gully (Route 41), Stob Coire nan Lochan, Glencoe. (Photo: Ken Crocket)

Stuart Smith on the Gash (Route 59), Bidean nam Bian, Glencoe.
(Photo: Ken Crocket)

25: AONACH EAGACH RIDGE (E, II/III) 8km

Summary: The narrowest, most difficult ridge traverse on the mainland. Previous rock climbing experience advisable for a summer traverse (short rope useful). A winter traverse is far more serious — start early, carry a rope and a few slings, and avoid delays.

First Ascent: A.R. Wilson, A.W. Russell and A. Fraser, August 1895.

Best Conditions: In summer, choose any clear day free of strong winds. Conditions in winter are very variable and the route is best avoided when verglassed rock or deep powder snow are present. Firm snow, though rare, will give the most enjoyable conditions. Check weather forecasts carefully; the ridge has no intermediate descents by which to escape in unexpected bad weather.

Approach: Along the A82.

Starting Point: At a small car park at GR:174 567, a few hundred metres west of Allt-na-reigh cottage. To begin the traverse, either ascend directly up the South-East Ridge of Am Bodach, or cross this ridge into the confined eastern coire and gain the main ridge at GR:172 582.

Descent: In good visibility, continue 500m west from the last top, Sgorr nam Fiannaidh (967m, GR:141 583), then descend south over steep grass. Avoid the badly-eroded descent path on the west side of Clachaig Gully. Alternatively, continue the traverse to the unnamed west top of Sgorr nam Fiannaidh, then turn north-west towards the Pap of Glencoe (742m, GR:125 594), finally descending by easy slopes.

The Aonach Eagach, or 'Notched Ridge', stretches unbroken along the north side of Glencoe. Its flanks are seamed with gullies and defended by steep slopes of the worst kind, but in summer its pinnacled crest gives a pleasurable day's walking and scrambling, and in winter a fine expedition on narrow snow crests.

Difficulties, summer or winter, are concentrated at the 20m descent from Am Bodach, and on a pinnacled section between Meall Dearg and Stob Coire Leith. Views down to the twisting road far below enhance the sense of elevation.

The Reverend A.E. Robertson, the first person to ascend all the Munros, saved the Aonach Eagach until last. On reaching the summit of his final Munro, he is reliably reported to have kissed first the cairn, then his wife!

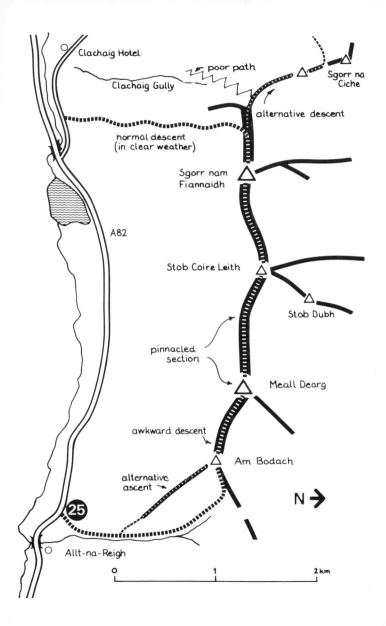

Clachaig Hotel

poor path

Clachaig Gully

Sgorr na
Ciche

alternative descent

normal descent
(in clear weather)

Sgorr nam
Fiannaidh

A82

Stob Coire Leith

Stob Dubh

pinnacled
section

Meall Dearg

awkward descent

Am Bodach

alternative
ascent

25

Allt-na-Reigh

N →

0   1   2 km

26: CURVED RIDGE (M, II/III) 240m

Summary: An entertaining route, and in summer a suitable introduction to rock climbing for the fit beginner. In winter it serves to introduce the more technical winter buttress climbs. Excellent rock, with plenty of stances. (Illustrated in more detail on Route 27 diagram.)

First Ascent: Summer — G.B. Gibbs, July 1896. Winter — G.T. Glover and R.G. Napier, April 1898.

Best Conditions: Dries quickly in summer and is usually snow-free from April to October. Should be climbable at any time of the winter season, given sufficient snow cover (but avoid during bad weather, when the descent will be uncomfortable, if not dangerous).

Approach: (1) The Jacksonville path (refer to Route 27 approach), or (2) The Lagangarbh path (convenient for those wishing to descend via Coire na Tulaich): leave the road at Altnafeadh (GR:222 564), cross the River Coupall by a footbridge, and pass Lagangarbh. Now follow the path left, rising gently, to converge with the Jacksonville path at the Waterslide Slab. Go up left of the Waterslide Slab to reach the lowest rocks, then make a rising rightward traverse to emerge at the foot of a gully system (the lower stretches of Easy Gully), which is flanked on the right by the Rannoch Wall. 1hr (perhaps 1hr 30mins in winter).

Starting Point: At the right side of the base of the ridge, and left of the foot of the scree or snow-filled gully system, at an altitude of 630m.

Descent: If visibility is poor, follow these directions to avoid an unintentional descent into Glen Etive.

From the summit of the Buachaille (Stob Dearg, 1022m), go 270m along the level summit ridge on a bearing of 250 degrees magnetic. Now descend uncomplicated slopes for 270m on a bearing of 270 degrees magnetic to gain the col at a height of 870m. Turn north and descend via Coire na Tulaich. The upper slopes of the coire are fairly steep but uncomplicated.

In summer the rough rhyolite of Curved Ridge gives an enjoyable ascent of surprising variety. The views of the surrounding country lend poignancy to reflective moments, while the impressive rock scenery closer at hand — including the spectacular climbers' playground of Rannoch Wall — provides a dramatic setting for the action.

The ridge has two easy sections: near the start, and about half-way up. A section of steeper rock after each of these will require more thought.

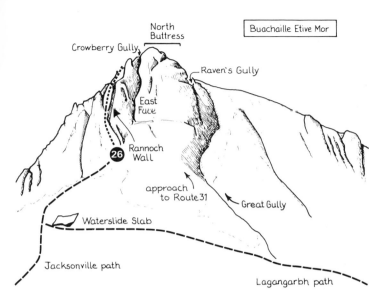

There is more scope for variation in the upper reaches. In winter, diversions into Easy Gully could be made to avoid awkward pitches on the ridge itself.

The final steep section of the ridge consists of short walls and chimneys. It ends abruptly at a cairn near the finish of Easy Gully, just below the base of Crowberry Tower. The actual summit of Stob Dearg lies about 75m above. In summer, scramble easily up to it from the termination of the ridge; in winter, traverse about 30m left to a snow slope and exit up the left-hand of two wide gullies above.

27: AGAG'S GROOVE (VD) 105m

Summary: A justly popular classic which follows a soaring fault line on the Rannoch Wall. Good protection balances a big atmosphere. Tremendous exposure and outlook.

First Ascent: J.H. Hamilton, A. Anderson and A.C.D. Small, August 1936.

Best Conditions: Faces east at an altitude of 600m. Should dry quickly after rain during the period April to October.

Approach: (1) The Lagangarbh path (refer to Route 26 approach), or (2) The Jacksonville path: start from an unmarked car park at GR:236 554, 1km west of the junction between the A82 and the Glen Etive road. Cross the River Coupall (difficult after heavy rain) and pass by the Jacksonville hut. Now head directly uphill to pass the left side of the prominent Waterslide Slab (junction with the Lagangarbh path). Continue as for Route 26 until opposite the foot of the Rannoch Wall. 1hr 15 mins.

Starting Point: At the far right-hand side of the face, at a crack behind a detached, rectangular block.

Descent: The route finishes on Crowberry Ridge. Scramble up this to below the Crowberry Tower at 900m. From here a path leads leftwards to the large cairn at the top of Curved Ridge. Descend the ridge to the starting point.

Agag's Groove was only the second route to breach this great, red wall. It was a fine prize for the first ascent party, which had reached the rocks just minutes before Bill MacKenzie's rival JMCS party.

Climbers who today follow the clean, well-marked rock can be forgiven their ignorance of its original mossy and muddy state. Leading the first ascent, 'Hamish' Hamilton was forced to wear socks to help combat greasy rock encountered on the crux bulge of what is now the third pitch.

The climbing, open yet secure, is divided into three sections: corner, groove, and wall. A difficult move in the corner of the first pitch is probably the technical crux, while the exposed nose on Pitch 3 is the steepest. The rock is good apart from a few loose blocks near the top of the wall — a minor blemish on an impressive route. Rarely is it possible to experience such situations at this grade.

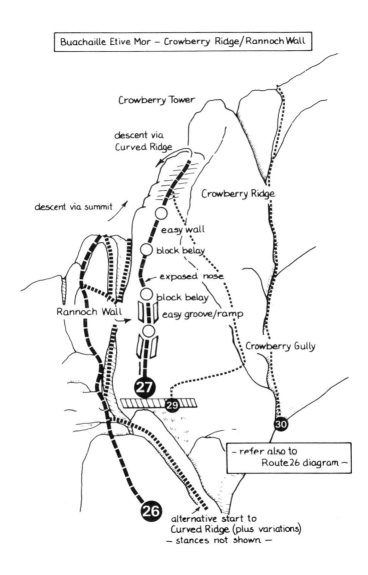

Buachaille Etive Mor – Crowberry Ridge/Rannoch Wall

Crowberry Tower

descent via
Curved Ridge

Crowberry Ridge

descent via summit

easy wall

block belay

exposed nose

Rannoch Wall

block belay

easy groove/ramp

Crowberry Gully

27

29

30

– refer also to
Route 26 diagram –

26

alternative start to
Curved Ridge (plus variations)
– stances not shown –

28: WHORTLEBERRY WALL (VS+) 120m

Summary: An exposed and potentially serious wall climb which almost warrants the *HVS* grade. For the leader, the crux arrives at the top of the poorly-protected first pitch. The upper traverse pitches will make demands of their own on the rest of the team. Uncertainty of outcome and striking situations add to the route's stature.

First Ascent: J. Cunningham and W. Smith, September 1956.

Best Conditions: Faces east at an altitude of 600m. Best months, April to October.

Approach: (1) The Lagangarbh path (refer to Route 26 approach), or (2) The Jacksonville path (refer to Route 27 approach). Follow Curved Ridge (Route 26) until opposite the foot of the Rannoch Wall. 1hr 15mins.

Starting Point: The gully at the foot of the Rannoch Wall (Easy Gully) contains two pitches, the first of them a cave. Start between the two, about 20m above the cave pitch and below the middle of an obvious red slab.

Descent: As for Route 27 (up to Crowberry Tower; follow a path leftwards to the cairn above Curved Ridge; down Curved Ridge to the starting point).

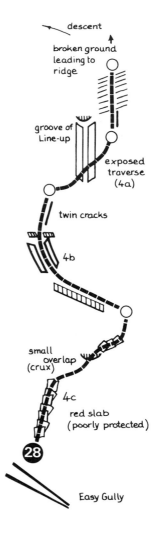

descent

broken ground leading to ridge

groove of Line-up

exposed traverse (4a)

twin cracks

4b

small overlap (crux)

4c

red slab (poorly protected)

28

Easy Gully

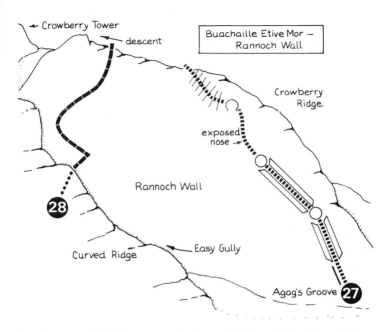

Cunningham and Smith, two ace climbers of the Creagh Dhu Club, climbed the beautiful red slab almost ten years before their complete ascent. They named their audacious pitch 'Autumn Slab'. Nowadays it is possible to find five or six protection placements on this pitch, but they are of doubtful worth. Towards the top of the red slab is a smaller, raised slab which must be traversed before reaching easy rock and a belay. A lengthy and committing stride across this raised slab proves to be the crux.

Two traverses follow — first left, then right — in a manoeuvre which flanks the bulging wall above the first stance. On the third pitch (by which time the exposure has reached awesome proportions), the direct but damp corner of Line-Up is avoided by continuing the traverse on good holds to reach easy ground beyond.

29: NAISMITH'S ROUTE (III) 210m

Summary: A classic buttress route, the seriousness of which modern technology can do little to ease. Ascends the easiest line up Crowberry Ridge, following for the most part a shallow gully just right of the true crest.

First Ascent: Winter — not known. Summer — W.W. Naismith and W. Douglas, August 1896.

Best Conditions: What little ice might form here would probably be a nuisance, and conditions of hard snow are infrequent. The best one can hope for is reasonable snow cover and a windless day, not too early in the season.

Approach: As for Route 26 to the foot of Easy Gully. Climb Easy Gully to the foot of a 6m chimney at the very foot of the Rannoch Wall. The chimney leads easily to a terrace on the right (the First Platform).

Starting Point: Below the chimney, or at the right end of the First Platform near Crowberry Gully, on the left-hand side of a 15m pinnacle (which is not obvious from below).

Descent: Continue to the summit as for Curved Ridge (Route 26) and descend as for that route (but refer to descent notes for Route 30).

The first main pitch follows the Abraham brothers' direct route up a shallow chimney on the pinnacle's left side. This takes one to Pinnacle Ledge. Above is Abraham's Ledge, with the infamous crux of the direct route to its left. Instead, we follow Naismith and make a short traverse right to enter the leftmost of three shallow chimneys. The angle relents somewhat after a few steep moves in the chimney, and a shallow gully with a few small steps is entered. Ignore the awesome drop into Crowberry Gully on the right as you approach a sloping slab — if you can!

Conditions decide the best place to quit the slab for the crest of Crowberry Ridge on the left. In poor conditions this may be a lower traverse from the foot of the slab, but there can be no hard and fast ruling. Once on the ridge, easy slabs and an easy ridge lead in 75m to the base of the Crowberry Tower. An exposed path leads left from here to the cairn of Curved Ridge, up which the route finishes.

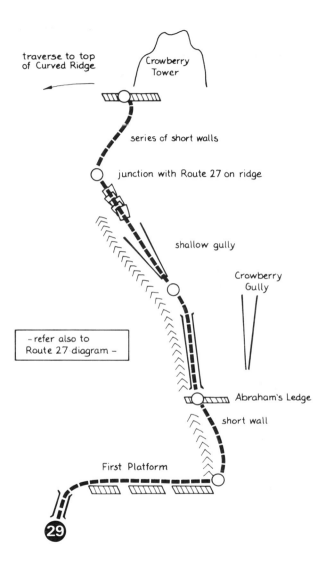

traverse to top
of Curved Ridge

Crowberry
Tower

series of short walls

junction with Route 27 on ridge

shallow gully

Crowberry
Gully

- refer also to
Route 27 diagram -

Abraham's Ledge

short wall

First Platform

29

30: CROWBERRY GULLY (III/IV) 300m

Summary: A long, classic gully in impressive surroundings. Often in condition. There may be several minor pitches in addition to the usual three distinct pitches. Deadmen useful. Start early and, depending on experience and competence, consider soloing or moving together on the initial snow pitches to save time.

First Ascent: Winter — H. Raeburn, W.A. Brigg and H.S. Tucker, April 1909.

Best Conditions: Normally in condition from the end of January onwards, although a harder ascent in thinner conditions may be possible earlier in the season. If snow and ice in the gully appear continuous from the road then the route is probably climbable (except when avalanche conditions prevail).

Approach: As for Route 26 to the foot of the gully system. The left fork of the system leads into Easy Gully and the right fork into Crowberry Gully.

Starting Point: At the entrance to the gully, adjacent to the rocks of Crowberry Ridge.

Descent: As for Route 26. However, if conditions on top are thought to be very bad, a competent party may effect a descent via Curved Ridge itself (Route 26).

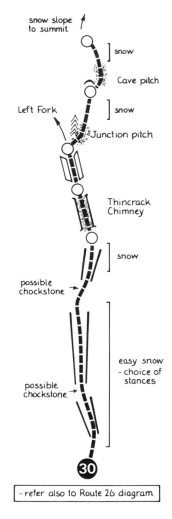

snow slope to summit

snow

Cave pitch

snow

Left Fork

Junction pitch

Thincrack Chimney

snow

possible chockstone

easy snow - choice of stances

possible chockstone

30

- refer also to Route 26 diagram

Crowberry Gully (originally Gully B), received its first ascent by Harold Raeburn in April 1898. However, the ascent was 'disallowed' because 'mixed' conditions prevailed (snow pitches alternated with those of rock). Historians still argue the case. No-one could question the quantity of snow present during the first recognised ascent — Raeburn and party were avalanched!

Initial, easy snow pitches lead to a minor pitch at a chockstone (obscured in good conditions). Several more snow pitches, best climbed up the left side to take advantage of sheltered belays under the rock wall, lead to the first hard pitch — the Thincrack Chimney. In winter this may be the hardest pitch, as the rocky slab on the right is invariably thinly iced with few holds. Bridging works best here, supplemented by a few front-point placements for the left foot in the corner itself. You might find a thread runner in the depths of the corner, but don't waste time searching if it isn't obvious.

A rock rib parts the gully into Left and Right Forks. This is the Junction. Unless looking for very hard times, traverse right, close under the rib, and climb up to easier and deeper snow in the Right Fork. Bold climbers may find it easier to descend slightly from the belay and traverse on to the convex wall of the slab where the ice is thicker.

A long pitch on snow should just reach a fine stance in the Cave (there is usually a peg high on its left wall). The final difficulty — the short but steep wall of the Cave Pitch — lies ahead. During busy periods this will have been hammered and kicked until the way is obvious. It begins with a rightward traverse from the Cave, until it is possible to move up more directly. The angle relents after 10 – 12m and the thankful leader will be able to continue more easily in a snow groove. A long run-out (losing communications) leads either to a rock belay immediately under, or a snow belay immediately above, the finish of the gully. A short snow slope now leads up and right to the summit — an appropriate finish to one of Scotland's classic winter gullies.

31:   BOTTLENECK CHIMNEY (S) 40m

Summary: A short but interesting route with strenuous jamming and a subterranean exit. Unusual climbing for Glencoe. Hard for its grade.

First Ascent: R.G. Donaldson and G.R.B. McCarter, Summer 1941.

Best Conditions: A short gully drains into the chimney; the route requires several days of good weather to dry out after rain.

Approach: (1) Via the Jacksonville path (refer to Route 27) to Curved Ridge, followed by a rightward traverse to below the two-tier 90m crag of the East Face of North Buttress, or (2) begin via the Lagangarbh path (refer to Route 26), but leave it before reaching the Waterslide Slab and take to the lowest rocks of the North Buttress, which are easiest on the left. 1hr 20mins.

Starting Point: A broad ledge, the Terrace, extends below the face. It terminates on the right at a projecting rock rib. Start 6m left of the rib at a dark recess.

Descent: Traverse right, then go down the easy rocks of North Buttress until it is possible to traverse back left to regain the Terrace.

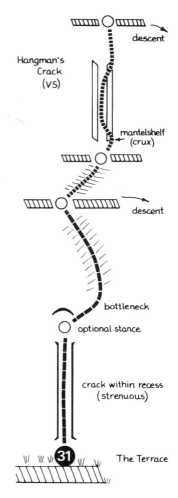

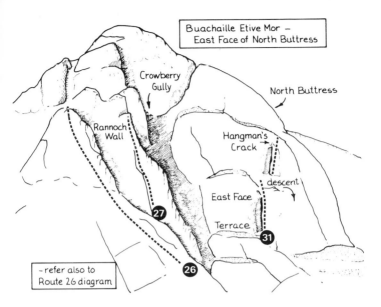

Crowberry
Gully

North Buttress

Rannoch
Wall

Hangman's
Crack

descent

East Face

Terrace

27

31

26

- refer also to
Route 26 diagram

The obvious deep recess of Bottleneck Chimney can be plainly seen even
from the road. The name is partly a misnomer; on closer inspection it
proves to be a recess containing a crack.

An ability to bridge and jam is a positive asset on the strenuous first 20m.
Fortunately the protection is good, and there is a resting place at its top in
an unusual cave-like recess. Some climbers may choose to take an
intermediate belay here to avoid possible rope-drag later.

The next section involves overcoming the 'bottleneck' — a narrowing on
the right gained by a high traverse under the arch. Release is as sudden as
a popping champagne cork. Thereafter, all that remain are the easy rocks
of a shallow scoop.

The first ascent party continued up the next tier by the corner of
Hangman's Crack (VS), but many will avoid it by escaping rightwards on to
the North Buttress descent.

32: RAVEN'S GULLY (V) 180m

Summary: Despite its age (it is now over 35!), this episodic gully maintains its grade and character. It is a confined and complex climb, with several strenuous chockstone pitches to outwit. Cunning and experience count as much as boldness here, where the skills required for success can have more to do with climbing rock than snow and ice.

First Ascent: H. MacInnes and C.J.S. Bonington, February 1953.

Best Conditions: This is no place to be during a thaw or falling snow. Be patient and wait for a period of consolidation, hopefully near the end of the season when there will be more daylight hours. February and March are the most promising months.

Approach: By the Lagangarbh path. Leave the A82 at Altnafeadh (GR:222 564), cross the River Coupall footbridge, and turn left after passing Lagangarbh (SMC hut). The path rises gently to cross the slabby chasm of Great Gully. From here there are two alternatives, depending on conditions. If Great Gully is well banked-up, and safe, it may be possible to follow this route. Otherwise, ascend slopes just left of the gully, and then contour into it below Slime Wall. 1hr 30mins.

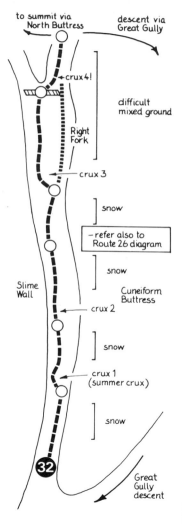

Starting Point: At the foot of the gully which defines the right-hand side of Slime Wall.

Descent: If conditions allow, traverse right from the top of the route and descend a shelf leading back to Great Gully. If this gully is in avalanche condition (as is often the case), go left from the top of the route and ascend to the summit by the easy rocks of North Buttress (descend as for Route 26).

Hard-men will solo the first pitch, which is an easy one leading to the giant chockstone. Now fight for the right to occupy the stance underneath it (there is a good thread at the back) to be sure of reserving the summer crux for your hapless partner.

Don't waste time looking for holds on the chockstone itself; instead, concentrate on the left wall. There are no real holds here either, but with applied concentration the front points just might grip the rock long enough for a pick to be jammed higher up in the corner between wall and chockstone. Brute strength is better than artistry in coping with this problem, although tired muscles will disagree when asked to complete the final moves to surmount the chockstone.

Snow leads to the second chockstone, which normally succumbs to back-and-footing. A step from the chockstone leads into another wicked groove (a speciality of Raven's Gully!), which some climbers believe to be the hardest winter pitch. In any case this deceptive and poorly-protected pitch deserves respect. An easier pitch above leads to the gully fork.

Those determined to have a very hard time of it might care to try the subterranean right fork, first climbed in winter by Chouinard and Tompkins (February 1970), but most mortals will be satisfied with the normal finish. This climbs a wall and groove on the left before continuing up mixed ground to a large ledge and possible belay. The last pitch, the Corkscrew, rises from the right-hand end of the ledge. Yet another groove on the left side of a chockstone, this holdless and runnerless pitch will be climbed with friction, gulle, and not a little faith.

33: BLUDGER'S REVELATION (HVS) 130m

Summary: This combination of routes provides a long, sustained, but well-protected outing. A good introduction to the harder routes on this great face. The rock is rough but uncompromising, particularly in the lower reaches. Avoid a cold day!

First Ascent: Bludger's Route − P. Walsh, H. MacInnes and T. Lawrie, September 1952. Revelation − P. Walsh and C. Vigano, June 1956. Link Pitch − J.R. Marshall, J. Griffin, G. Adams and R. Marshall, July 1957.

Best Conditions: The route should dry after several days of good weather in the period April to October.

Approach: By the Lagangarbh path. Leave the A82 at Altnafeadh (GR:222 564), cross the River Coupall footbridge, and turn left after passing Lagangarbh (SMC hut). The path rises gently to cross the slabby chasm of Great Gully, where the path divides. Either climb slopes just left of the gully, before contouring into it below Slime Wall, or, more securely, climb rocks on the right side of Great Gully (until above a big pitch in the gully), and then cross into it below Great Gully Buttress. 1hr 30mins.

Starting Point: About 10m down and left of the foot of Raven's Gully, at a corner almost directly below the left-hand of two obvious, parallel grooves on the face.

Descent: Scramble up, then traverse right immediately above the finish of Raven's Gully. A sloping shelf descends into Great Gully. Descend the gully with care, keeping close in under Cuneiform Buttress, to regain the start.

The sustained enjoyment of a steep groove on the second pitch is matched by the original first pitch of Revelation − an exposed, rising traverse on wonderful, bubbly lava. The situations on the route are 'north face' in atmosphere, the dark cleft of Raven's Gully contrasting with the sunlit buttresses across the gully. The route belongs to Patsy Walsh of the Creagh Dhu, a strong man with severe myopia (he climbed several major variants during his career through failing to locate the original line!), who in one summer climbed no less than five routes on this face.

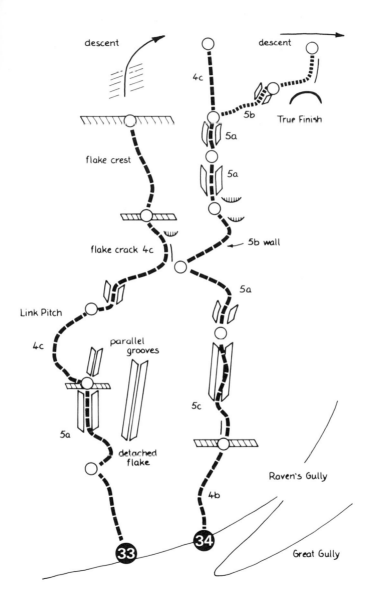

descent

descent

4c

5b

True Finish

5a

5a

flake crest

5b wall

flake crack 4c

Link Pitch

5a

4c

parallel grooves

5c

5a

detached flake

Raven's Gully

33

34

4b

Great Gully

34: SHIBBOLETH (E2) 190m

Summary: An ageless classic up the most imposing part of this barrel-fronted buttress. Takes first a prominent groove, then a baffling wall, in two sustained and committing pitches climbed on small holds. Protection on the rightward diagonal of Pitch 4 is minimal. (Illustrated on Route 33 diagram.)

First Ascent: R. Smith and A. Fraser, June 1958. Smith's True Finish − R. Smith and J. McLean, June 1959.

Best Conditions: An infamous weep on the second pitch crux is rarely, if ever, completely dry. Allow 3 or 4 days to dry (more after prolonged wet weather).

Approach: As for Route 33.

Starting Point: 6m below and left of the foot of Raven's Gully.

Descent: As for Route 33.

The young Smith was committed to raising the standards of Scottish rock climbing to equal those in England and Wales. In 1958, with the ascent of Shibboleth, he succeeded.

The route starts by the first pitch of an older and less demanding climb called Guerdon Grooves. A prominent member of the Creagh Dhu once announced: 'If you can't solo the first pitch, you shouldn't be trying Shibboleth!'

The main objective is a steep groove guarded on its left side by a black, weeping crack. The entry to this groove is the key to the route. It is gained by first going up the crack, then left, and finally up and right over the wet section. The groove is deceptively steep, its moves committing, but it slowly relents as the belay approaches.

The next pitch continues up the groove to a step right at its top. From there it goes up and left to take a belay below the Revelation flake.

The next section will be thought the crux by some. Small holds take one up and right for 15m before good holds appear. A traverse left leads to a stance below an overhang.

Two corner pitches above lead to a parting of the ways. The traditionalist will finish up the wall above, while those looking for hard ways will traverse right to a bottomless groove for Smith's True Finish − a strenuous wall traverse leading to a crack above a huge recess.

35: SPARTAN SLAB (VS) 190m

Summary: The most amenable route on a unique sweep of glassy granite. Sections of friction climbing are short, and the route is well protected. Most *VS* leaders will have a fighting chance of completing the route unscathed! (Illustrated on Route 36 diagram.)

First Ascent: E.D.G. Langmuir, M.J. O'Hara and J.A. Mallinson, June 1954.

Best Conditions: South facing at 300m. Allow 2 days of good weather after rain. Best period: March to October (although midges can be a serious problem during July and August).

Approach: Refer to Glencoe area map and follow the winding Glen Etive road. This is single track, with passing places, and leads in 23km to the road-end parking area at an old pier on Loch Etive (GR:097 446). From here the path leads diagonally across the hillside, arriving at the foot of the main slab near a large block (cheerfully known as the Coffinstone). 40mins.

Starting Point: 5m left of the Coffinstone, below a right-trending groove with heather.

Descent: The route finishes just below the descent path: follow it carefully down to the right (take care not to dislodge stones), cross a shallow watercourse, then descend to regain the foot of the slabs.

The first two pitches trend right to gain a ledge and tree. On the left now is an overhung recess − a horrid granitic problem of crushing simplicity, climbed (usually) with thrashing knees. It leads to a huge, semi-detached block − the Crevasse. The horizontal crack above leads rightwards to a tree belay near the edge of the slab.

A cracked groove on the right leads to another thin crack in a steeper slab on the left, which in turn leads to good cracks above an overlap. Old peg scars now provide the holds in what originally must have been a difficult pitch, requiring pegs for aid. Cracks, blocks and a chimney lead easily in two pitches to a heathery finish.

Depending on the climber's thrutching ability, the crux will be either the overhung recess or the cracks of the fifth pitch. Pegs are no longer required for protection now that chockstones can be fitted into the old peg holes.

36: SWASTIKA (E1) 200m

Summary: A bold route following an amazing quartz band in the centre of the main slab. Not for the faint-hearted. The main overlap contrasts sharply with the two crucial and unprotected slab pitches which follow. The old aid section on the upper part is now climbed free to give the route its technical crux.

First Ascent: M. Noon and E. Taylor, June 1957.

Best Conditions: As for Route 35 (March — October, allow 2 dry days; midge problem July — August).

Approach: As for Route 35 (Glen Etive road from A82; park at road-end; diagonal path to main slab). 40mins.

Starting Point: From the Coffin-stone, follow the path leftwards at the foot of the slabs for 40m, passing a large silver birch, to below a clean slab. Start below the right-hand of two parallel cracks.

Descent: As for Route 35 (path down to right).

Swastika takes a fairly direct line up the main slabs, deviating only to traverse the Moustache — the grass-encrusted edge of the overlap which cuts across the main slab. No pegs are required for aid, nor should they be placed for runners as the rock is unable to withstand sustained damage.

The first section leads to a belay below the huge overlap. This looks impregnable, but the gymnastic leader will find large holds on the overlap to fuel a foot-swing on to the ledge above. The hesitant will surely tire and fail. The second, threatened by the prospect of a huge pendulum, will appreciate a runner here.

An easy but exposed 'walk' along the Moustache leads to a stance. The quartz band pitches follow; runnerless tiptoeing up tiny pink steps with not a single runner to soothe fraying nerves. The second quartz band leads to a stance under the second main overlap.

The next section consists of a short overhanging corner on the left, a slab under a tree, and the old aid pitch just left of the main crack. This will severely tax fingers and arms, thus far unworked. Beyond that are just two short corners, then heather and sweet release.

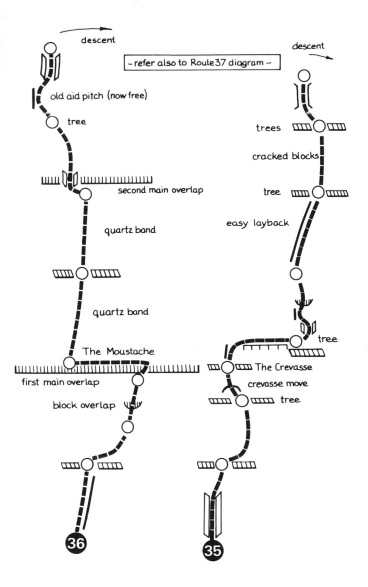

descent

- refer also to Route 37 diagram -

descent

old aid pitch (now free)

tree

trees

cracked blocks

tree

easy layback

second main overlap

quartz band

quartz band

tree

The Moustache

The Crevasse

first main overlap

crevasse move

block overlap

tree

36

35

37: HAMMER (HVS) 190m

Summary: A sustained route based on a major corner feature. The climbing is surprisingly varied, with a mixture of corner laybacks and delicate slabs. Both cruxes arrive on slab sections, but with better protection than usually found on the main slab routes.

First Ascent: M. Noon and J. Cunningham, April 1957.

Best Conditions: As for Route 35 (March — October, allow 2 dry days; midge problem July — August).

Approach: As for Route 35 (Glen Etive road from A82; park at road-end; diagonal path to main slab). 40mins.

Starting Point: Follow the path up left from the Coffinstone, passing one corner (Agony), to gain the foot of the second main corner line by an easy scramble.

Descent: As for Route 35 (path down to right).

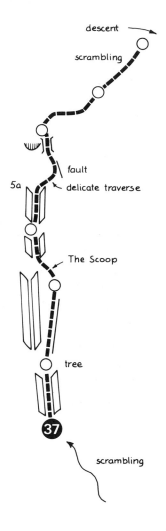

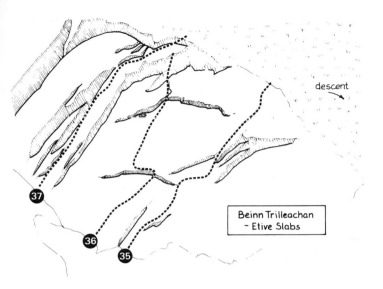

descent

Beinn Trilleachan
– Etive Slabs

A corner pitch and cracked slab lead to the stance below the first crux. This is the famous Scoop, a shallow fold in the granite slab which guards re-entry into the corner. It succumbs to a sequence of committing friction moves. To hesitate is to join the growing band of leaders who have faltered and gracefully slid back down to the stance. The corner leads to a stance below the second crux.

20m above the stance you will hope to find an old peg (and if hopes are dashed then try to arrange some nut protection), because this is where the rightward tension traverse used to begin. 'Used to' is the key phrase; now it is climbed free, making the best of tiny edges to reach a fault in the slab. The next objective is the overhang at the top of the slab. The bemused leader, recently glad to have gained some holds (however small), now realises that the holds continue to be small and the protection continues to be absent. The overhang arrives just when it looks as though the pitch is about to turn sinister; a move right, then up, leads to a stance at the end of the major difficulties.

38: SCABBARD CHIMNEY (IV) 120m

Summary: An intriguing, if relatively obscure, winter climb based on a summer *Severe*. Provides a heady mixture of snow grooves and difficult buttress climbing.

First Ascent: L.S. Lovat, J.R. Marshall and A.H. Hendry, February 1956.

Best Conditions: The climb holds very little ice, and so hard snow provides the best conditions. These are rare. Nevertheless, the route does hold snow reasonably well, and so a good freeze after a few days of gentle thaw could produce the desired results.

Approach: As for Route 47 to the coire. Now head for a point just right of the lowest rocks of Summit Buttress, and left of Broad Gully. 2hrs.

Starting Point: Below a chimney which slants up to the right, under the steep right flank of Summit Buttress.

Descent: From the summit, descend the North Ridge to reach the top of Broad Gully. When in safe condition, this gully provides an easy descent with no pitches. However, if avalanche conditions are suspected, continue traversing the ridge northwards to reach easy slopes beyond Pinnacle Buttress. Descend these to the coire floor.

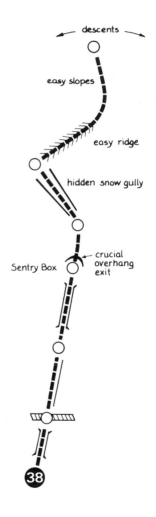

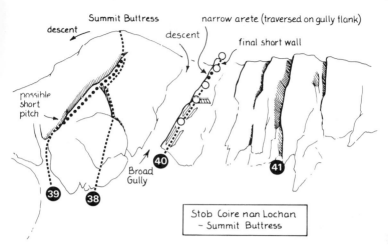

Stob Coire nan Lochan
– Summit Buttress

The initial chimney leads easily to a ledge below the summer slab. This will probably be impossible in winter, forcing the climber into a steep crack on the left. It was here that one resourceful leader, stranded without footholds just below the top, hammered a deadman across the fissure to make a perfect footplate!

The next pitch is superb — a well-protected crack and chimney on the buttress wall. The angle is steep, but holds are good. It eases and leads into a sentry box below the crux — an overhang above the belay.

Depending on conditions and pick placements, several strenuous moves will be needed before easier mixed ground above the crux can be gained. Some parties have had to resort to combined tactics here, and in any case the second ought to be fully prepared for the possibility of a leader fall. After the crux, and some climbing up the corner continuation, the route suffers an abrupt change in character. Here a snow gully darts suddenly up to the left, emerging on the easy summit rocks of the buttress.

39: BOOMERANG GULLY (II) 210m

Summary: A pleasant and un-complicated route, winding its way through broken rocks to the summit of Stob Coire nan Lochan. Normally a straightforward ascent on snow, although it may include one small pitch. (Illustrated on Route 38 diagram.)

First Ascent: J. Black, R.G. Donaldson and W.H. Murray, January 1949.

Best Conditions: These cliffs rise above the 800m level and provide the most reliable con-ditions in Glencoe (upper section visible from the roadside). A good cover of firm snow is best for this route, although most winter months should provide enough snow for an ascent (excluding times when avalanche conditions prevail).

Approach: As for Route 47 to the coire. On the left of the coire stands the bulky Summit Buttress, with steep rocks on the right flank, and more broken ground on the left. 2hrs.

Starting Point: From a point below and left of the steepest rocks of the buttress, where a snow slope will be seen rising up and slightly left.

Descent: (1) Continue to Bidean nam Bian. (2) Down the east ridge, bending north-east, to gain the ridge of Gearr Aonach. (3) As for Route 38 (down Broad Gully; or, if avalanche conditions prevail, continue northwards along ridge to descend beyond Pinnacle Buttress).

The curving line of Boomerang Gully proved irresistible to W.H. Murray and his companions (Murray was at this time busy writing the first *Climbers' Guide to Glencoe*). But for the war it would almost certainly have been recorded earlier.

As its name suggests, the gully is well defined, and there are no route-finding problems. The route simply starts at the foot of the obvious snow gully and follows the logical line.

The distinctive rightward bend of the gully is not visible from below. At this point there may be a small pitch. Above, the gully gradually opens out and leads on to the final ridge. This in turn leads to the summit of Stob Coire nan Lochan, with grand views east to the Buachailles of Etive, and the Rannoch Moor beyond.

40: DORSAL ARETE (II) 120m

Summary: An enjoyable and satisfying buttress climb in magnificent surroundings. The line becomes better defined as height is gained. There is no distinct crux. Useful in conditions of heavy snow, when gully climbs are best avoided. Good belays throughout. (Illustrated on Route 38 diagram.)

First Ascent: J. Black, T. Shepherd, J. Allingham and J. Bradburn, January 1951.

Best Conditions: Climbable under almost any type of snow cover. Normally in condition from December onwards. Long slings and nuts are useful.

Approach: As for Route 47 to the coire. Now head towards the rocks just right of the foot of Broad Gully. 2hrs.

Starting Point: At the foot of Broad Gully, on the left side of the rib of rock.

Descent: Go left and descend to reach the top of Broad Gully. When in safe condition, this provides an easy descent with no pitches. However, if avalanche conditions are suspected, traverse the ridge northwards from the top of the climb to reach easy slopes beyond Pinnacle Buttress. Descend these to the coire floor.

The art of safe winter climbing is adjusting the plans according to conditions. If ambitions are set on a classic gully on Stob Coire, then obviously a certain amount of determination is required. But unsafe conditions call for discretion. The gully will still be there next year — but will you? A buttress climb is often safe when a gully is not, and on such a day there is no better choice than Dorsal Arete.

A shallow groove will be found on the buttress, leading up in two pitches to an obvious ledge. The next pitch leads to the abrupt narrowing of the arete — the dorsal fin — with steep drops on either side. Many climbers avoid the actual fin (which at its narrowest is no wider than a boot's length) by traversing under its left flank. Either way the final wall at the top of the fin will soon be reached. A high step-up here gains the finishing moves in excellent position.

41: SC GULLY (III) 150m

Summary: One of the two classic gully climbs of the coire. Superb rock architecture. Modern equipment in the right hands will make short work of it in good conditions, but anything can happen when the crux pitch is thinly iced. A cornice may add to the difficulties. Deadman useful.

First Ascent: P.D. Baird, E.J.A. Leslie and H.A. Fynes-Clinton, March 1934.

Best Conditions: A reasonable cover of snow and ice is required, particularly on the crux pitch. Avoid thaw conditions, or times of shifting snow (such as after recent snowfall).

Approach: As for Route 47 to the coire. Now head for the gully between South and Central Buttresses. 2hrs.

Starting Point: At the foot of the gully, left of the lowest rocks of Central Buttress.

Descent: (1) Go left to descend Broad Gully as for Route 40. (2) If Broad Gully is found to be in avalanche condition then you should not have been in SC Gully! Anyway, count yourself lucky and instead traverse the North Ridge to easy ground beyond Pinnacle Buttress.

Such was the effort required to climb ice during step-cutting days that the first ascent party avoided the first small ice pitch in favour of a rib on the left. The modern first pitch confronts the ice, continues up snow, and enters a closed recess dominated by rock walls.

Escape from the recess is normally by an ice ramp in the right corner, gained by a short traverse. There will be a steep move or two before pulling over on to the ramp. If the ice is sufficiently thick, then the final section (of perhaps 70 degrees) will provide an airy but safe exercise. If, on the other hand, the ice is thin, you deserve every sympathy. In very lean conditions, when the crux ice pitch is incomplete, it is possible to effect an escape up the headwall in the left corner of the gully, although this will be harder than the normal route.

Once above the crux pitch, the difficulties should be over; uncomplicated snow will lead to the final headwall. This is rarely corniced, although it may steepen for a few metres.

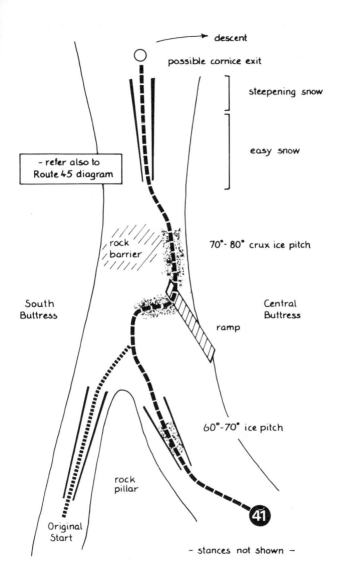

descent

possible cornice exit

steepening snow

easy snow

- refer also to
Route 45 diagram

rock
barrier

70°- 80° crux ice pitch

South
Buttress

Central
Buttress

ramp

60°- 70° ice pitch

rock
pillar

Original
Start

41

- stances not shown -

42: TWISTING GULLY (II/III) 150m

Summary: The second of the coire's two classic gully climbs, now hallowed by time and reputation. In fact more of a buttress climb than a gully, with an interesting crux pitch.

First Ascent: W.H. Murray, D. Scott and J.C. Simpson, December 1946.

Best Conditions: Any cover of snow in freezing conditions should suffice, unless loose snow is shifting down the buttress. A small snowfield in the upper section can avalanche in thaw conditions.

Usually in condition from January onwards.

Approach: As for Route 47 to the coire. Now head for the narrow gully immediately under the left flank of South Buttress. 2hrs.

Starting Point: At the foot of the gully (deadman, or possibly a rock belay, at its left side).

Descent: As for Route 40 (down Broad Gully; or, if avalanche conditions prevail, northwards along ridge to descend beyond Pinnacle Buttress).

The rock scenery is particularly impressive in the lower reaches of the gully, where the normal route shares its start of steep snow with the harder right fork. Good belays on the left wall secure the stance at the fork.

A chimney promises an exit up the left fork, but the line runs out at a bulge. The left wall itself, steep and smooth, appears to offer no better prospect. But note the ledge leading out left from half-way up the chimney. This is the escape route we have to take. Snow permitting, a good nut runner in the corner will protect a committing heave up on to the ledge. Once established, tall climbers will find themselves handicapped by the bulging wall above. Balance will be regained after a few leftward shuffling moves to the edge. This interesting pitch has a sting in its tail! A tiny rib above has to be overcome with an awkward, though protectable, mantelshelf.

A final small pitch can be awkward, but there is every incentive to succeed — it is the gateway to the summit. Easier snow above the pitch is climbed without complication, curving rightwards to the final slopes.

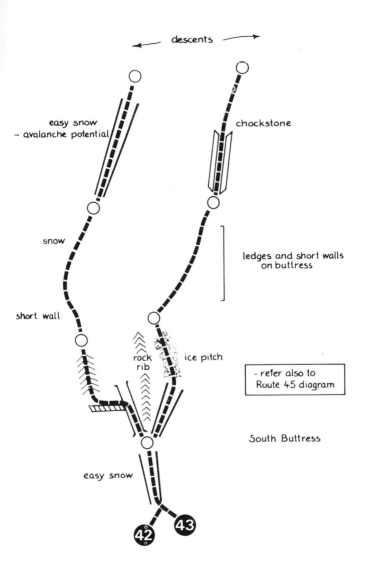

descents

easy snow
– avalanche potential

chockstone

snow

ledges and short walls
on buttress

short wall

rock
rib

ice pitch

- refer also to
Route 45 diagram

South Buttress

easy snow

42   43

43: MOONSHADOW (III/IV) 150m

Summary: A good natural line, well seen from the approach, taking the prominent corner high on the left flank of South Buttress. Mixed ice and buttress climbing. Sustained and enjoyable to the last move. (Illustrated on Route 42 diagram.)

First Ascent: K.V. Crocket and C. Stead, January 1972. Right fork pitch — J.R. Marshall and I.D. Haig, January 1958.

Best Conditions: A good plastering of snow is preferred, while a period of frost is required to build ice on the original right fork pitch (the state of this pitch may determine overall success or failure).

Approach: As for Route 47 to the coire. Now head for the narrow gully on the left flank of South Buttress. 2hrs.

Starting Point: At the foot of the gully, as for Route 42 (deadman, or possibly a rock belay, at its left side).

Descent: As for Route 40 (down Broad Gully; or, if avalanche conditions prevail, northwards along ridge to descend beyond Pinnacle Buttress).

The first pitch, common with Twisting Gully, climbs the deep cleft on easy snow to the rib which divides the gully. Twisting Gully goes left, while this route takes the steep ice pitch in the right corner.

In step-cutting days this pitch seemed always to consist of the most glutinous and resistant ice, but of course this is now recognised as being ideal material for front-pointing. A modern leader will romp up this pitch when it is heavily iced. The belay is about 10m above the top of the pitch, below the corner on the buttress.

A pitch on the right wall now takes in a series of small ledges as it zigzags up the buttress, eventually finding a thread belay in the corner. From below it now looks as if an impasse has been reached, but closer inspection reveals a narrow groove running up to the left. An obvious, jammed chockstone will provide a suitable runner and rest. You will pop out on top of the buttress not far above this chockstone, perhaps startling some unsuspecting passer-by (if not yourself).

44: ORDINARY ROUTE (III/IV) 150m

Summary: No 'ordinary route' at all! (Look at the first ascent date.) A sustained buttress climb with fine positions — a climb to savour on a good day.

First Ascent: H. Raeburn, Dr and Mrs C. Inglis Clark, April 1907.

Best Conditions: Gauge conditions from the state of the first steep pitch on the coire face; if this has sufficient material, then so should the remainder of the buttress. An ascent later in the season has the advantage of extra daylight.

Approach: As for Route 47 to the coire. Now head for Central Buttress. 2hrs.

Starting Point: Refer to Route 45 diagram.

Descent: As for Route 40 (down Broad Gully; or, if avalanche conditions prevail, northwards along ridge to descend beyond Pinnacle Buttress).

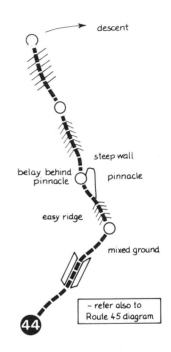

The vegetated bay taken by the first section benefits from the smothering effects of winter. Above a corner, you will move right to gain the ridge crest and a welcome belay. The route now follows the crest for a short distance to a tower (prominent from below). This is overcome via a chimney on the right. Remaining difficulties centre on a series of short but baffling walls. Exposure on the right adds atmosphere.

45: CENTRAL GROOVES (VS) 120m

Summary: Climbs the conspicuous corner of Central Buttress set amid wild and scenic surroundings. Sustained and unusually steep for the grade. Persevere when things look desperate — holds do appear!

First Ascent: K. Bryan and R. Robb, July 1960.

Best Conditions: This is a high crag, set at an altitude of 1000m, and so requires 2 or 3 days of good weather to dry out. Best months: May to September.

Approach: As for Route 47 to the coire. Now head directly up towards Central Buttress. 2hrs.

Starting Point: Below the obvious groove, just left of the buttress crest. There is a small roof on the crest at 5m.

Descent: From the top of the buttress, go left to reach the top of Broad Gully and descend this into the coire. There are no pitches in the gully, but loose scree demands care. Alternatively, turn right and go down the ridge until beyond Pinnacle Buttress. Easy slopes then lead down into the coire.

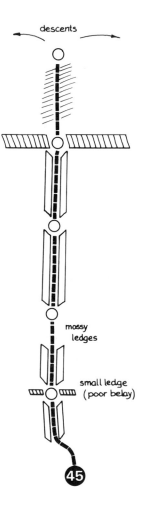

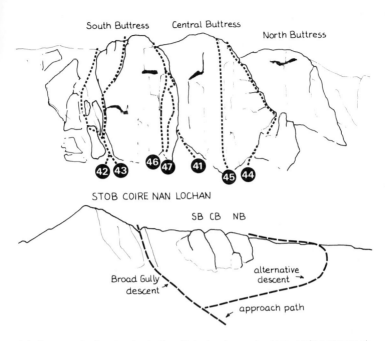

South Buttress   Central Buttress   North Buttress

42 43   46 47   41   45 44

STOB COIRE NAN LOCHAN

SB CB NB

alternative descent →

Broad Gully descent ↗

approach path ←

A bulge guards direct entry to the pitch, forcing a short traversing approach from below and to the right. A committing swing on a good hold gains the corner, which in turn leads to small ledges and a poor belay.

The corner shoots straight up from here, leading to moss-covered ledges which cut across the buttress. A downward glance from this point reveals the start of the climb, so direct is the line it follows.

Three sections on the corners and grooves which follow provide distinct problems, but all are well protected. Route-finding is as straightforward as you would expect, although some parties have been known to traverse too far left on the upper section of the buttress.

46: UNICORN (E1) 110m

Summary: A modern classic in a magnificent setting, following the huge corner near the right edge of the buttress. One of the very best climbs in Glencoe. Although the route is not high in the grade, the first pitch is surprisingly technical, involving poorly-protected friction bridging on its holdless sections.

First Ascent: J.R. Marshall and R.N. Campbell, June 1967.

Best Conditions: This is a high crag, set at an altitude of 1000m, and so requires 2 or 3 days of good weather to dry out. Best months: May to September.

Approach: As for Route 47 to the foot of the South Buttress. 2hrs.

Starting Point: Near the right edge of the buttress, at a narrow grass ledge beneath the prominent corner.

Descent: As for Route 45 (left along ridge and then down Broad Gully; or right, until beyond Pinnacle Buttress, and then down easy slopes leading to the coire floor).

The corner of the first pitch is a technical delight. Try bridging, back-and-footing, or any other technique that results in upward progress! You can be sure that the lack of protection for the first 7m will add a sense of urgency to your efforts.

A move right now brings the rib and more conventional climbing within reach. It leads in 6m to a high handhold and runner. This protects the hard moves required to regain the corner and better holds. A block once facilitated the moves left, until one day it objected to some rough handling and decided to detach itself, almost annihilating the second who waited below.

The remainder of the corner line is sheer delight, climbing good andesite in a magnificent mountain setting. After three pitches, the route emerges on to the crest of the buttress at tottering blocks. But the route has a sting in its tail — directly ahead lies the final corner with its deep jamming and one hard move.

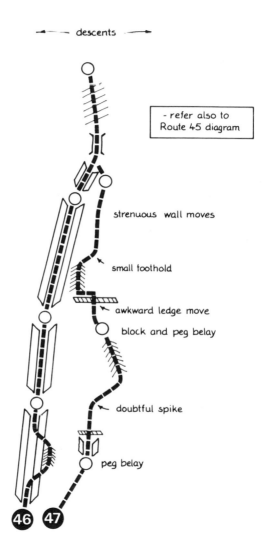

descents

- refer also to
Route 45 diagram

strenuous wall moves

small foothold

awkward ledge move
block and peg belay

doubtful spike

peg belay

46 47

47: SCANSOR (E2) 100m

Summary: A bold and impressive line, taking the leaning pillar immediately right of the Unicorn corner. Sustained, exposed climbing with some strenuous moves. Superlative surroundings and rock architecture. (Illustrated on Route 46 diagram.)

First Ascent: P. Braithwaite and G. Cohen, September 1972.

Best Conditions: This is a high crag, set at an altitude of 1000m, and so requires 2 or 3 days of good weather to dry out. Best months: May to September.

Approach: Descend from a parking area on the south side of the A82 (GR:169 569) to cross the River Coe by the footbridge at GR:166 566, about 1km downstream from the Meeting of the Three Waters. The path, which is well marked, leads up and around into the glen below the cliffs of the East Face of Aonach Dubh (seen above on the right). The path crosses the burn higher up the glen and leads into the delightful pot coire. Thread through the boulder field in the coire floor, then scramble up grass to the ledge below South Buttress. 2 hrs.

Starting Point: As for Route 46.

Descent: As for Route 45 (left along ridge and then down Broad Gully; or right, until beyond Pinnacle Buttress, and then down easy slopes leading to the coire floor).

The route begins up the rib that forms the right edge of Unicorn corner; it is gained by a short pitch to a ledge at 6m. The second pitch is a full run-out, first following the obvious corner to a small ledge. The wall above leads to a peg runner and doubtful spike. This marks the start of a rightward traverse to the steep arete, which in turn leads to a block belay.

The third pitch begins awkwardly in an attempt to gain an upper ledge on the left. While enjoying the few moves on the left arete, you might pass the time in conversation with climbers half-way up Unicorn! When ready, a rightward traverse leads to a small foothold in the centre of the pillar. From here some strenuous moves lead up right to a ledge and junction with Unicorn. Now only a short chimney separates you from easy rocks and deserved elation.

48: WEEPING WALL ROUTE (S) 105m

Summary: A sustained climb on small holds, typical of Glencoe, following a cracked fault up a bulging wall.

First Ascent: D. Scott and J.C. Henderson, August 1947.

Best Conditions: Requires up to 2 days' drying time (April to October).

Approach: As for Route 49 to below the lowest crag on the east face — the Weeping Wall. A useful landmark is a large fallen block at the foot of the wall, about 12m left of the right edge of the face. 50mins.

Starting Point: Just left of the fallen block.

Descent: Scramble up to the Terrace, traverse it leftwards, and then descend the Lower Bow.

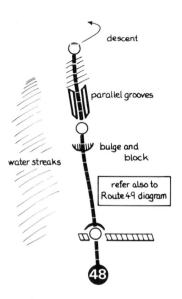

Weeping Wall Route is probably the best of three *Severes* which lie in close proximity on this face. To get an overall picture of the line, stand back from the face and look for a left-trending cracked fault (a short pitch leads to a belay in a recess below it). The fault pitch ends with a bulge and block climbed directly. Finally, parallel grooves, which are climbed by the line of least resistance, lead to easier ground.

The route is not a memorable one in terms of this or that move. Instead it imprints character with a steady flow of good, sustained climbing. Connoisseurs of wall routes will understand.

49: QUIVER RIB (D) 60m

Summary: Follows a clean rib and grooved wall on good holds. Unusually steep and exposed for the grade. Excellent rock.

First Ascent: D.B. McIntyre and W.H. Murray, May 1947.

Best Conditions: Dries quickly within the period late spring to early autumn, although some of the large holds on the steep section store rain-water for some time after!

Approach: Descend from a parking area on the south side of the A82 (GR:169 569) to cross the River Coe by the footbridge at GR:166 566, about 1km downstream from the Meeting of the Three Waters. The path, which is well marked, leads up and around into the glen below the cliffs of the east face (seen above on the right). Continue along the path until opposite the main face; alternatively, cross the burn at a lower level, above a small waterfall. Just left of the middle of the main face is a small outcrop with rowan trees — a convenient stopping point. Behind this rises a long, shallow groove — the Lower Bow (*M*) — which serves as a useful access route to the Terrace. Climb the Bow to reach the Terrace. 1hr 20 mins.

Starting Point: A dark, wet chimney limits the left side of the Terrace Face. Start below the rib, immediately right of the chimney.

Descent: As for Route 51.

The pleasant first rib is savoured as a starter for the main course — a steep wall indented by a narrow groove which soars up to the left. This does not look promising, but after one difficult move above the stance, the tension evaporates with the discovery of a series of huge holds.

Bill Murray did not have the benefit of this knowledge when belaying at the midway ledge during the first ascent. While watching McIntyre's lead of the steep section, he grew so worried by the possible outcome that he lost faith in his existing belay and began to search for something better! But his fears were unfounded; McIntyre completed the pitch without mishap. Only later, while following the pitch, did Murray discover for himself the true nature of the climbing.

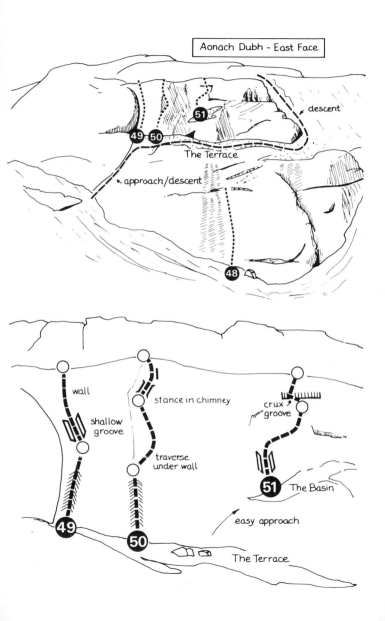

Aonach Dubh - East Face

descent

The Terrace

approach/descent

wall

shallow groove

stance in chimney

crux groove

traverse under wall

The Basin

easy approach

The Terrace

50: ARCHER RIDGE (VD) 65m

Summary: The route follows a sinuous line up a blunt ridge with steadily increasing difficulty. Hard for the grade. Grooves on the left side of the ridge are generally turned by short rightward traverses. Mistakes with route-finding are punished by harder and steeper rock. (Illustrated on Route 49 diagram.)

First Ascent: W.H. Murray and D.B. McIntyre, May 1947.

Best Conditions: Dries quickly after rain within the period late spring to early autumn.

Approach: As for Route 49 to the Terrace. 1hr 20mins.

Starting Point: A damp chimney defines the left end of the Terrace. The steep wall to its right ends at a blunt ridge. Start at the foot of the ridge.

Descent: As Route 51.

It seems likely that the Creagh Dhu had climbed several lines on this face before Murray and McIntyre recorded their climbs of May 1947. But this hardly detracts from the legacy of fine routes which have since become so popular.

Their campaign opened with the bow-shaped chimney which defines the left side of the main face. To the right of its upper part they noticed a ridge which was as straight as an archer's back. The top section looked impossible, but, encouraged by their recent experiences on Quiver Rib, when holds appeared when most needed, they resolved to attempt the line.

The first pitch of rough rock led the pioneers up the crest of the ridge (where nowadays the runners, though few, are adequate). They failed to climb the steep corner groove directly above the stance, which is often wet and now climbed by a harder variation, and avoided it with a dog-leg to the right before returning to the crest.

The route up the final impending wall from their corner stance lay through the obvious breach. It involved pull-ups on awkward holds − a strenuous manoeuvre now thankfully well protected − but it won them ultimate success.

51: HESITATION (HVS) 60m

Summary: A two pitch climb of sustained interest and an unforgiving crux. Delicate climbing below contrasts with the impressive roof traverse and crucial break-out. (Illustrated on Route 49 diagram.)

First Ascent: J. Cunningham, July 1966.

Best Conditions: Requires up to two days' drying time (April to October).

Approach: As for Route 49 to the Terrace. Enter the lush hollow in the centre of the Terrace Face, the Basin, from the left. 1hr 30mins.

Starting Point: At a belay above and left of the trees in the Basin, and below a shallow groove which itself is just left of a slabby scoop.

Descent: From the top of the Terrace Face, go right to gain a two-tier chimney. Descend the first chimney on the outside, and the second on the inside. Descend further and then turn under the Terrace Face, heading diagonally down the Terrace to gain the top of the Lower Bow. Descend this to regain the outcrop and rowan trees at the foot of the main face. In clear weather, an alternative descent may be found down slopes to the right of the crag.

This route will test your resolution right from the beginning, the luxuriously-vegetated Basin makes an excellent sun-trap! But the first pitch beckons. It lies up a shallow, though obvious, groove in the slabby wall. The scoop just to its right — The Gut (*VS*) — was climbed by Cunningham, with Bill Smith, ten years before his Hesitation ascent. A traverse right from a ledge above the groove leads to a tiny stance shared with The Gut, which goes right from here.

The next pitch is the crux — a 5m leftward traverse under the roof to a break-out right by an awkward, overhanging groove. Cunningham used a peg for aid here on the first ascent. Now it is climbed free by some committing moves. Difficulties soon ease, however, and the large ledge above provides a good belay.

Presumably the second could not, or would not, follow Cunningham's lead up this short but action-packed route.

52: BOOMERANG (VS) 90m

Summary: Climbs the most prominent feature on the face — a corner crack. The crux responds to some committed bridging and finger-jamming. Hard for its grade.

First Ascent: J. Cunningham and M. Noon, August 1955.

Best Conditions: Requires 2 or 3 days to dry out after rain. Best period: April to October.

Approach: As for Route 49 to below the East Face. Cross the burn just above a small waterfall. Now head up to the right, over grassy slopes, to gain the foot of the crag which overlooks the entrance to the glen. 50mins.

Starting Point: Near the left end of the pale wall, below the left curving corner.

Descent: From the finish, go left above the crag to descend grass slopes. Finally, pass back under the face to regain the starting point.

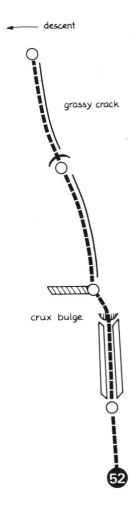

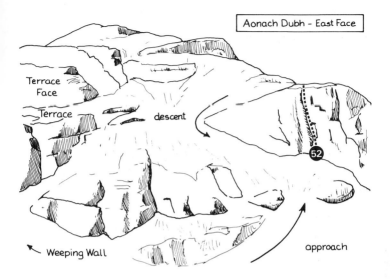

Terrace
Face

Terrace   descent

52

← Weeping Wall   approach

Boomerang was climbed by members of the Creagh Dhu club in a year when many of the classic *VS* routes on the Buachaille were being recorded. Its uncompromising line and character gave them a route of distinction.

A short pitch up the wall leads to a stance under the crack. Some unscrupulous leaders will conveniently neglect to stop here, hogging the best of the route by climbing the wall and crack in one run-out.

The crack gradually steepens until it begins gently to overhang. This is the crux. A few strenuous moves lead to a step left and salvation at a belay ledge. Doubtless the reach of 'Long' John Cunningham came in useful here! Difficulties are now over as the climb opens out into two easy crack pitches leading to the top.

53: YO-YO (E1) 90m

Summary: Follows a stunning corner line in three, well-protected pitches. Direct, strenuous, and uncompromising.

First Ascent: R. Smith and D. Hughes, May 1959.

Best Conditions: Receives little sunshine and may require 3 or 4 days to dry out. Best months: April to October.

Approach: Descend from a parking area on the south side of the A82 (GR:169 569) to cross the River Coe by the footbridge at GR:166 566, about 1km downstream from the Meeting of the Three Waters. Now head up and right to gain the Sloping Shelf, a prominent feature which slants across the entire North Face from middle left to top right. Follow the Shelf up right, crossing an awkward gully, until below the upper cliffs (the Shelf continues to the bottom of Deep-Gash Gully). 1hr 40mins.

Starting Point: Half-way along the buttress wall left of Deep-Gash Gully, below the great vertical corner.

Descent: Follow the Pleasant Terrace ledge system down to the right to reach a chimney. Descend the chimney to enter a wide, shallow fault. The fault leads down to Sloping Shelf at a point just left of Deep-Gash Gully.

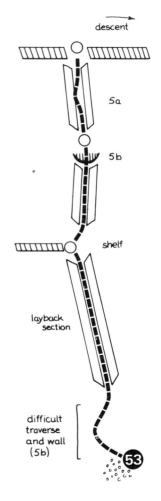

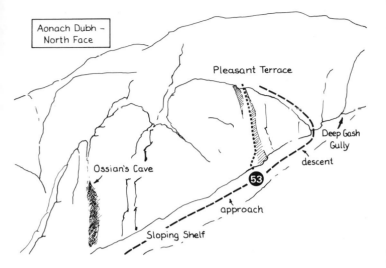

Aonach Dubh –
North Face

Pleasant Terrace

Deep Gash
Gully

descent

53

Ossian's Cave

approach

Sloping Shelf

The line of Yo-Yo can be seen from the road. It has instant appeal, and for some climbers the ascent of its great corner becomes an obsession. Whillans attempted it in the dead of winter, December 1955. Not surprisingly the adverse conditions beat him back from the difficult section a few metres above the start. But Smith also had to work hard for this line, clearing away moss and other offending vegetation.

Technically, the crux is the devious first 6m or so above the rattling scree of Sloping Shelf. But having gained the corner, a delightful layback on easing rock leads to a shelf and belay.

The middle pitch is brutal. A 12m crack leads to a widening below an overhang, climbed over chockstones with gradually increasing exposure. The route overhangs in two dimensions, and a fall would leave the leader suspended in space.

The third and final pitch takes the continuation crack with one or two minor deviations to the left (but ignore a left-trending ramp above half-height and instead exit to Pleasant Terrace via the final groove). This deceptively strenuous finish sometimes proves the downfall of tired leaders.

54: THE BIG TOP (HVS) 150m

Summary: Another Smith classic. Interesting route-finding and a strenuous crux. Exposed.

First Ascent: R. Smith and J. Gardiner, August 1961.

Best Conditions: Requires about 2 days of good weather to dry after rain. Best months: April to October.

Approach: From the junction of the A82 and the old road leading to the Clachaig Inn (GR:137 566). Cross a stile at the south-west corner of the bridge, and follow the obvious path leading to Coire nam Beith. Leave it below the lowest waterfall, and go left, crossing the burn, to gain Dinner-Time Buttress. Ascend to Middle Ledge and traverse it rightwards to reach E Buttress, which is left of the deeply-cut No.4 Gully.

Starting Point: On Middle Ledge, at a block belay below the right edge of the buttress' West Face.

Descent: Descend an easy ramp rightwards to enter No.4 Gully. Descend this with care, scrambling down steep ribs in the gully bed, to regain Middle Ledge.

The route begins by slanting up left to a slabby corner, before trending back right to a large flake below an overhang. The next pitch takes the bulging arete on the right, testing commitment with an exposed move, before a crack leads to an easement.

Now begins the rising traverse across a grooved wall overlooking the slab of Trapeze — a fine *E1* climbed by Marshall in the summer of 1960. The rock looks dubious, but it is comforting to know that no-one seems to have parted company with this section of the climb (there's always a first time . . .). Detailed route-finding here is a problem for the leader, but at the end of the traverse look out for a 3m crack leading to a ledge below a huge flake.

The last, crucial pitch looms overhead. Smith's 'monster' flake leads to a steep wall, climbed first left then right. Above is an overhung groove, while to the right, and slightly below, is a slab. It is important to place a good runner in the groove before moving right. That done, a strenuous few moves gain the slab and a finish up the easing groove.

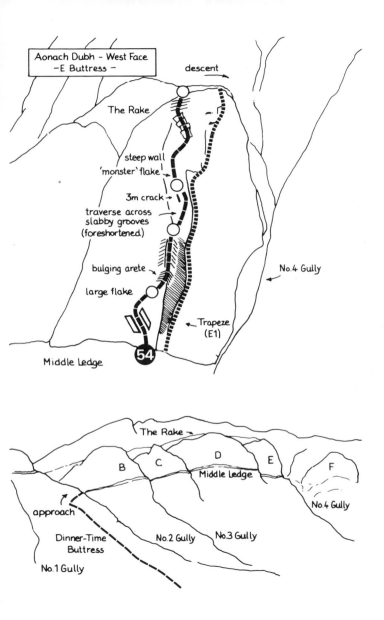

Aonach Dubh – West Face
– E Buttress –

descent

The Rake

steep wall
'monster' flake

3m crack →

traverse across
slabby grooves
(foreshortened)

bulging arete

large flake

No.4 Gully

Trapeze
(E1)

54

Middle Ledge

The Rake →

B   C   D   E   F

Middle Ledge

No.4 Gully

approach

Dinner-Time
Buttress

No.1 Gully

No.2 Gully   No.3 Gully

55: NUMBER SIX GULLY (IV) 240m

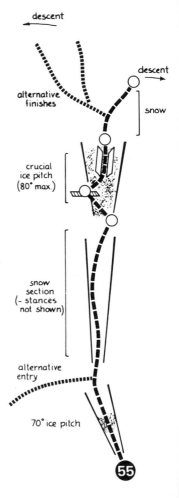

Summary: The best winter route on the face. Longer and harder than Crowberry Gully in typical conditions. Most of the difficulties are concentrated in one long ice pitch. Deadman useful.

First Ascent: D.H. Munro and P.D. Smith, March 1951.

Best Conditions: Requires a good freeze. The gully is at a lower altitude than most winter routes in Glencoe, and is therefore more susceptible to avalanche during a thaw. It can be seen from the road, from where likely conditions may be judged.

Approach: Initially as for Route 54, but continue up the Coire nam Beith path until above its steep section. Now cross over towards the West Face by the easiest line. 1hr 20mins.

Starting Point: At the foot of the gully (refer to diagram).

Descent: (1) If conditions and visibility allow, traverse rightwards from the finish to descend a shelf leading to the path in Coire nam Beith, or (2) continue up easier slopes to reach the ridge. Now go left to the top of Dinner-Time Buttress (gained via the easy upper section of No.2 Gully), and descend this to regain the approach.

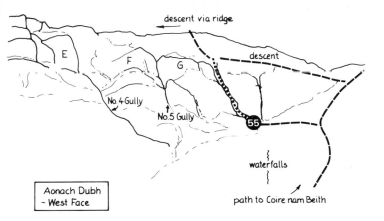

descent via ridge

descent

E F G

No.4 Gully

No.5 Gully

55

waterfalls

path to Coire nam Beith

Aonach Dubh
- West Face

The gully begins with a bang — a 10m ice pitch set at 70 degrees. Good for warming up cold arms. In an exceptional winter, however, it may be all but banked out. Above that, snow banked at a friendly angle lulls the climber into an easy frame of mind (which a tiny pitch at a sudden narrowing will not shatter).

A ledge running out to the left marks the end of the loose and easy-angled andesite, and the start of the rhyolite. Above and slightly left of the belay is a two-tiered 45m ice pitch. This is the crux. In places it will attain an angle of 80 degrees. First it is climbed up to the left, to a small ledge, then more steeply by a corner on the right (it may be best to split the pitch at the ledge, as belays are hard to find above).

Unless conditions are particularly icy, snow will now intervene before the gully rears up again to its trio of exits. The left exit is easy, while the centre is hardest. Take your choice depending on conditions, strength, and nerve.

56: SUMMIT GULLY (I/II) 450m

Summary: An uncomplicated snow gully, finishing close to the summit. There may be a small pitch near the start, and a small (avoidable) cave pitch higher up. Those intending to climb the route in pitches will find deadmen useful for belays. (Illustrated on Route 58 diagram.)

First Ascent: Not known (probably prior to 1910).

Best Conditions: If the snow is continuous, and not in avalanche condition, then the gully is climbable. Due to its length, however, it is best to wait for firm snow.

Approach: From the junction of the A82 and the old road leading to the Clachaig Inn (GR:137 566). Cross a stile at the south-west corner of the bridge, and follow the obvious path leading into Coire nam Beith. Continue alongside the Allt Coire nam Beith (awkward when icy) to the fork in the path. Cross the burn, and continue over slabby rocks to reach the boulder field in the coire below the face. The conical shape of the Stob Coire nam Beith can hinder route identification. Seen from the approach, Summit Gully is the obvious line beginning just left of the lowest rocks on the right-hand side of the face.

Starting Point: At the foot of the gully.

Descent: Descend the West Ridge from the summit to the col between Stob Coire nam Beith and An t-Sron. Now descend into the coire below the face.

Summit Gully is one of the longest in the area. Enclosing rocks add to the sense of scale. On a sunny day, with firm snow underfoot and blue skies above, the atmosphere here will be alpine. However, some parties have ended up on An t-Sron while searching for the gully in mist! (Careful map-reading should prevent this mistake.)

Although the gully trends generally left towards the summit, it begins with an open slope going up and slightly to the right. Soon after, it settles down to follow a well-defined line between buttresses. Higher up you might encounter a cave pitch; this can be climbed directly or turned on the right.

57: NORTH-WEST GULLY (II/III) 450m

Summary: A long, scenic gully. Pleasant and, taken by its original line, largely uncomplicated. Direct pitches of up to grade *IV* may form left of the normal start in a good winter, and there is an optional right-hand finish. (Illustrated on Route 58 diagram.)

First Ascent: G.F. Glover and R.W. Worsdell, April 1906.

Best Conditions: The route should be climbable under almost any depth of snow, but avoid periods following heavy snowfall. February and March will offer the best opportunities.

Approach: As for Summit Gully (Route 56) to the boulder field below the face. Summit Gully is the most obvious gully seen from the approach. The next gully to its left, beyond an intervening buttress (the Pyramid) is the shallow North-West Gully.

Starting Point: Below the Pyramid, at the indistinct beginnings of the gully just to its left.

Descent: The gully proper finishes at a convergence of buttresses, some distance from the top. From here there are two alternatives. Either: (1) continue easily to the summit and descend as for Route 56, or, if time is short, (2) traverse left above the finish of Arch Gully to enter the subsidiary coire between Bidean nam Bian and Stob Coire nam Beith. This is practical only if the traverse can be positively identified, and if visibility is good.

There is scope for much variation in North-West Gully. By its original and easiest line it is simply a matter of finding the start and pursuing the left-trending line. However, good conditions provide an opportunity to add an extra pitch or two at grade *IV* to the left of the usual start, joining up with the normal route later.

At the half-way fork, where the normal route goes left, there is another opportunity for variation (*III/IV*): take the right-hand branch, climbing for about 80m up the left side of a buttress called the Sphinx, to a second fork. Now fork left, climbing a short pitch on to a shoulder. A steep wall on the left of the shoulder — the culmination of five hours of step-cutting by the pioneers during the first ascent — may prove to be the crux.

58: DEEP-CUT CHIMNEY (III/IV) 450m

Summary: A classic ice gully, narrow and confined. The slot contains several ice pitches which are variable in length and difficulty, according to conditions. An additional 300m of easier buttress climbing beyond the amphitheatre is optional.

First Ascent: W.M. MacKenzie and W.H. Murray, April 1939.

Best Conditions: February and March offer the best chance of finding good conditions.

Approach: As for Summit Gully (Route 56), to the boulder field below the face.

Starting Point: Refer to diagram opposite.

Descent: (1) If time is short, traverse left from above the amphitheatre exit — crossing above Arch Gully — to gain a small, subsidiary coire between Stob Coire nam Beith and Bidean nam Bian. However, this route is practical only if it can be positively identified, and if visibility is good, otherwise (2) continue easily to the summit then descend as for Route 56.

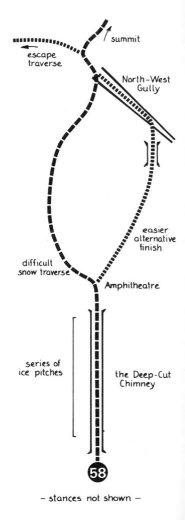

- stances not shown -

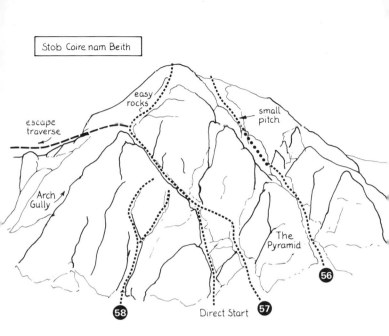

Stob Coire nam Beith

easy rocks

small pitch

escape traverse

Arch Gully

The Pyramid

56

58

Direct Start

57

In its day, Deep-Cut Chimney was considered to be one of the hardest winter climbs in the area, although not, in the opinion of some, as hard as Shelf Route on Crowberry Ridge, which had been climbed two years earlier by the same team.

One of the fascinations of winter climbing is the variability of conditions. Ice smears encountered on some routes in December or January may bank out completely with snow-ice later in the season. Deep-Cut Chimney is such a route, and only the most general comments can be made about the nature of its difficulties.

The initial deep slot contains the major difficulties. Normally these amount to several ice pitches of between 5m and 20m in length. A small amphitheatre above the last, and perhaps hardest, pitch has two exits. The true exit forks left, but if thinly covered then the right fork offers an easier alternative.

59: THE GASH (III/IV) 120m

Summary: An exciting and scenic climb, well worth the long approach march. Includes three good pitches in a narrow, slanting runnel. Good protection.

First Ascent: I.S. Clough, M. Hadley and M. Large, March 1959.

Best Conditions: The route carries no drainage, consequently there will be little ice build-up. For this reason, and despite an altitude of 1000m, the route can be wiped out in a thaw.

Approach: As for Route 56 to the coire below Stob Coire nam Beith. Continue, entering the higher coire under Bidean nam Bian itself. The West Top lies between the summits of those two mountains — enter the small subsidiary coire, to the east of Stob Coire nam Beith, to approach its north face.

Starting Point: The obvious and easy Hourglass Gully (I) splits the summit rocks. Traverse left from its foot to reach the start of the chimney-gully line of The Gash.

Descent: Go right to the col between the West Top and Stob Coire nam Beith. Descend from here into the subsidiary coire, and so regain the approach route.

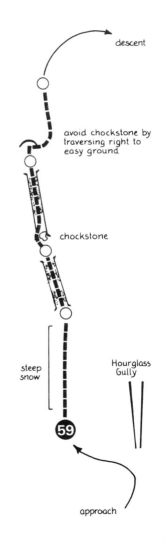

descent

avoid chockstone by traversing right to easy ground

chockstone

steep snow

Hourglass Gully

59

approach

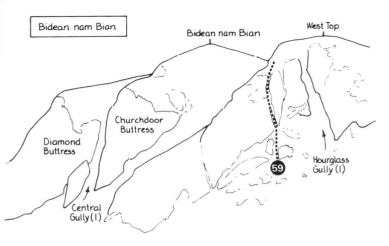

Bidean nam Bian

West Top

Churchdoor
Buttress

Diamond
Buttress

Hourglass
Gully (I)

Central
Gully (I)

59

There is something fascinating, and at the same time slightly frightening, about deep clefts like The Gash. The rock walls threaten, yet their very confinement can promote confidence, and whereas the lack of variation creates an air of predestination, which can be somewhat oppressive, it will at least simplify route-finding.

There will be no arguments about which line to follow. Standing on the small ledge at its foot, few will fail to be impressed by the soaring, straight-edged chimney line.

Hopefully there will be firm snow in the runnel of the first pitch. If so, a mixture of bridging and front-pointing should help to overcome its several bulges in a reasonably controlled and protected fashion.

At an overhanging chockstone, the left wall offers the only opportunity for escape. It will not be easy. Rumours have it that the next chockstone has a through-route at its back. That may be so, but most climbers will prefer a rightward traverse to reach easier ground and open spaces.

Ardgour Area

The area known as Ardgour and Sunart lies between Loch Sunart and Glen Tarbert in the south, and Loch Eil in the north. Loch Linnhe defines its eastern limit. Although no summit quite reaches the magic height of 3,000ft set by Munro, the area includes many beautiful mountains. Of most interest to rock climbers is the magnificent and aptly-named Garbh Bheinn — the 'rough hill'. It lies at an altitude of 898m, 2km north of Glen Tarbert and some 4.5km north-west of Inversanda. Its Great Ridge was climbed in 1897, but exploration was sporadic, and it was not until 1952 that a route was recorded on the great South Wall.

Ferry access ensures that Ardgour remains quiet. The climate is also favourable; it is often possible to climb on Garbh Bheinn while watching rain squalls hit Glencoe. Occasionally, clouds bearing West Coast drizzle will envelop the hills and remain for several days. Fortunately, the rock of Garbh Bheinn — a beautiful striped gneiss — remains wonderfully rough even when wet. Spring is easily the best time for a visit, when the weather is often better than commonly experienced in the height of summer. Stalking interferes with local access during the period September to February (enquiries at Inversanda House, GR:940 595).

Approaches: Leave the A82 Glasgow to Fort William road at the Corran Ferry (GR:022 635). This small car ferry operates only during daylight hours, and climbers are advised to make an early start in summer to avoid queues. The ferry can also be approached by bus from the south, or by train and bus via Fort William. The alternative to the ferry is a tedious drive north, along the A861 single-track road, to gain the A830 Mallaig road at the head of Loch Eil.

Accommodation: There are hotels on either side of the Corran Narrows. Campsites may easily be found along the shore of Loch Linnhe, thus avoiding confrontations with landowners.

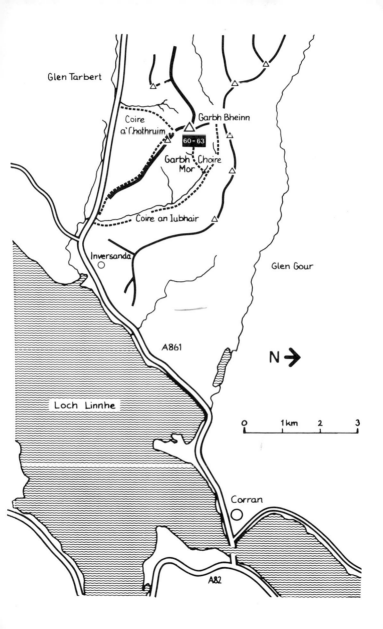

Glen Tarbert

Coire
a'Chothruim

Garbh Bheinn

60 - 63

Garbh Choire
Mor

Coire an Iubhair

Inversanda

Glen Gour

A861

N →

Loch Linnhe

0   1 km   2   3

Corran

A82

60: THE GREAT RIDGE (VD) 300m

Summary: One of the finest classical ridges, set in a quiet and scenic corner of the west coast. Varied climbing — slabs, walls, ridges — with one difficult section on the Direct Start. The rock is rough gneiss, and good holds abound.

First Ascent: Original route — J.H. Bell and W. Brown, April 1897. Direct Start — D.D. Stewart and D.N. Mill, April 1952.

Best Conditions: Spring can arrive early in Ardgour, so it is possible to enjoy the ridge in March. The upper part of the route dries quickly after rain, whereas the start may need two days. A visit during September or October may be frustrated by stalking.

Approach: From the Corran Ferry, follow the Strontian road (A861) to about 1km west of Inversanda (parking space at an old bridge, GR:928 596). Follow the path up Coire an Iubhair to the junction with the Garbh Choire Mor, then follow the less distinct path, through the narrow entrance, to the upper coire. The rocks of the Great Ridge will be seen ahead, bounded on the right by the deeply-cut Great Gully. 2hrs.

Starting Point: At the lowest rocks of the ridge, just right of a twisting crack, and below a steep slab.

Descent: Scramble south from the summit to reach the bealach at the head of the Garbh Choire. An easy descent can be made down the coire. More interestingly, climb with sacks and, from the bealach, continue south-east along the ridge, enjoying fine views down Loch Linnhe. The ridge, broken by numerous easy outcrops, leads back to the old bridge.

From the lowest rocks, a steep slab leads to a ramp. This slants up rightwards in two pitches, with one difficult step, to a grass ledge. A diversion to the left, around an edge, now leads up to another grass ledge below a chimney. Beyond the chimney, a rightward traverse gains the well-marked rocks of the original route with its satisfying final section. The route finishes dramatically on the summit of Garbh Bheinn (look out for a brass plaque below the actual summit), from where views to the east encompass the Glencoe hills.

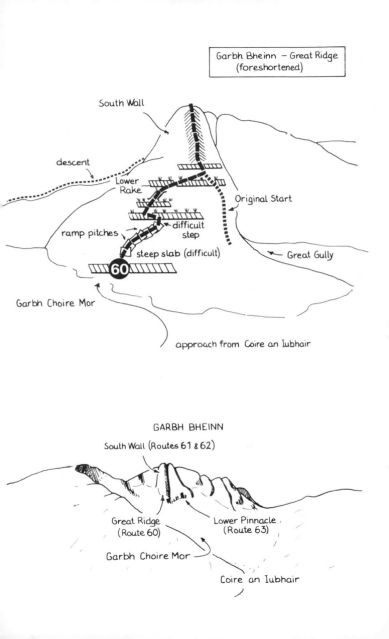

Garbh Bheinn — Great Ridge
(foreshortened)

South Wall

descent

Lower
Rake

Original Start

ramp pitches

difficult
step

steep slab (difficult)

60

Great Gully

Garbh Choire Mor

approach from Coire an Iubhair

GARBH BHEINN

South Wall (Routes 61 & 62)

Great Ridge
(Route 60)

Lower Pinnacle
(Route 63)

Garbh Choire Mor

Coire an Iubhair

61: BUTTERKNIFE (S +) 105m

Summary: Steep, sustained climbing in fine position, and on near-perfect rock, makes this one of the best *Severes* in the west of Scotland. The chimney and corner pitches are well-protected. High in its grade.

First Ascent: J.R. Marshall, A.H. Hendry, G.J. Ritchie and I.D. Haig, September 1956.

Best Conditions: The two-tiered South Wall catches the sun and may be climbable from March to October. This route takes a day or two to dry, however, depending on time of year and conditions. The first pitch may remain damp for longer.

Approach: (1) Via Coire an Iubhair, as for Route 60 (scenic but long), or (2) continue west on the A861 from the old bridge for a further 3km to reach the mouth of the next coire at GR:896 604. This is Coire a'Chothruim (unnamed on the 1:50,000 map). The path begins by following the east side of the burn, but soon fades. Proceed diagonally across the hillside — steep and heathery — to the bealach, south of the summit at GR:904 620. From the bealach, go up the ridge towards the summit until the sloping shelf under the South Wall can be seen. Descend this to the foot of the lower tier. 1hr 30 mins.

Starting Point: A huge boulder leans against the lowest point of the face. Immediately to its right is a large pillar of rock. There is a shallow chimney on its right flank. Start below the chimney.

Descent: From the summit, go a short distance west, then go south down the ridge to regain the top of the sloping shelf under the South Wall.

The chimney lends itself to a little gentle bridging, followed by a transfer to superb holds on the left wall. These lead to a good perch below the corner. This is climbed directly with some jamming and bridging — to give details would spoil the fun! From the belay at its top, two easy pitches lead to the terrace under the upper tier, arriving below an overhang at its far right end. A direct ascent of the upper tier gains the final, well-marked rocks of the Great Ridge.

Garbh Bheinn – South Wall

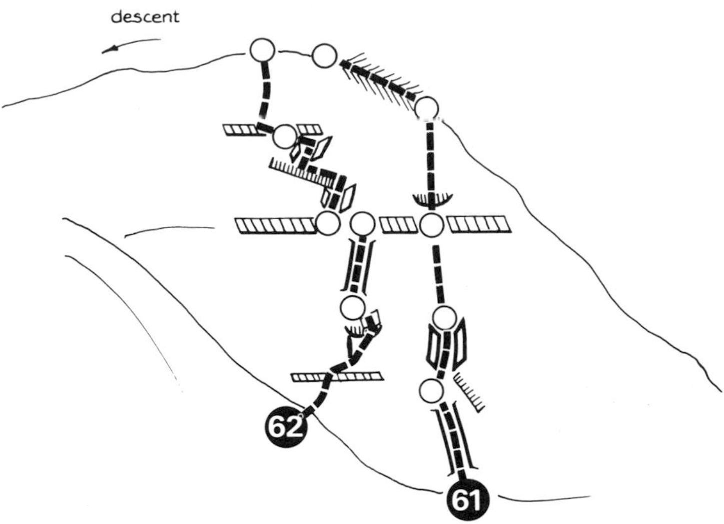

descent

62

61

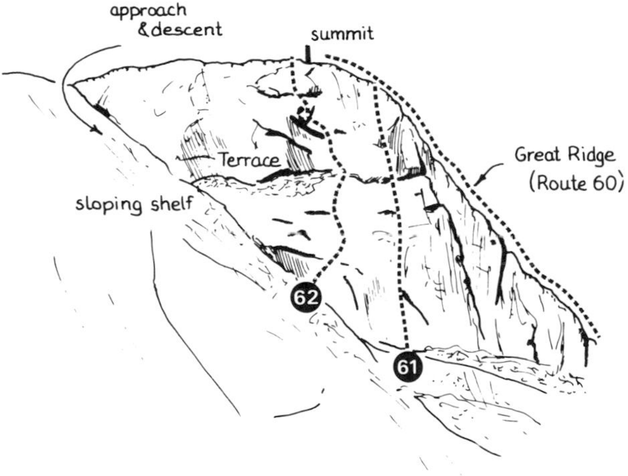

approach
&descent

summit

Terrace

sloping shelf

Great Ridge
(Route 60)

62

61

62: SCIMITAR/EXCALIBUR (VS +) 130m

Summary: This combination provides an exciting and sustained expedition up the centre of this great face. The route climbs both tiers of the South Wall, with a memorable traverse on each. (Illustrated on Route 61 diagram.)

First Ascent: Scimitar — D.D. Stewart and D.N. Mill, April 1952. Excalibur — K.V. Crocket and C. Stead. June 1972.

Best Conditions: Allow one or two days to dry (March to October).

Approach: As for Route 61.

Starting Point: A huge boulder leans against the lowest point of the face. About 30m left of the boulder, a shattered ledge curves up to the right. Begin at the start of this ledge.

Descent: As for Route 61.

The shattered ledge leads up to the right, and then lies back to the horizontal. From the left end of its horizontal section, a crack leads up steeply to an overhanging nose of rock. A step right in magnificent position (good holds) escapes the overhang, only to arrive at a delicate slab. Gingerly-executed moves lead up and left to a belay. An easier pitch gains the terrace below the upper tier.

Scimitar now continues up the upper tier by way of a smooth, vertical groove, but the climbing, though good, lacks the character of the preceding pitches. Excalibur makes a more fitting finish. It begins a few metres to the left, at a groove left of a yellow wall, and below the right end of the right-hand of two, prominent, slanting roofs.

The groove and rib to its right lead up to the start of the leftward traverse above the roof. Amazingly good, spiky holds abound. The traverse also has runner placements, but rope-pull may later lift these off (it takes a confident and capable second to follow this exposed traverse without full protection). The destination of this leftward excursion is a steeply-leaning corner. At its top, just as it threatens to overpower, a swing out left leads to a well-earned stance. Excitement over, the final pitch takes the upper wall, first slightly left, then straight up to the summit.

63: BLOCKHEAD (E1) 65m

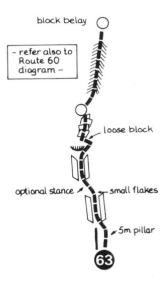

block belay

- refer also to
Route 60
diagram -

loose block

optional stance ←   → small flakes

↙ 5m pillar

63

Summary: A serious face climb. little known outside Scotland. Direct, uncompromising, and thoroughly typical of its originator.

First Ascent: R. Smith and V. Burton, March 1957.

Best Conditions: Requires two days to dry. Best period: March to October.

Approach: As for Route 59 into the Garbh Choire proper. Broken rocks right of the deep-cut Great Gully constitute the Winter Buttress; right again is the deceptively-named Pinnacle Ridge. This route takes the Lower Pinnacle. (Refer to Route 60 diagram.) 2 hrs.

Starting Point: At a 5m pillar, just right of the central crack on the front of the face.

Descent: Scramble down Pinnacle Ridge until it is possible to traverse across to regain the starting point.

Smith had yet to make his impact on Scottish climbing when he spotted this line. Very likely he bit off more than he could chew, but succeeded with typical determination and endurance.

The initial pillar is quitted below its top to a move left into a slim groove. At small flakes, a move left gains a shallow corner. It leads to a small overhang, turned on the right. A loose block on the left guards access to a recess, from where a slab on the right leads to a belay. Finally, the obvious arete above leads to the huge block belay which gives the route its name.

Ben Nevis

Ben Nevis, at 1344m the highest point in the UK, needs no general introduction here. Nevertheless, few of those who walk to the summit each year will see anything of the 3km of cliff on its North-East Face. This is hardly surprising — weather data culled from twenty-one years of continuous observation at the summit meteorological station (during the period 1883 – 1904) indicates that the chances of arriving on a cloud-free summit range from 50% in June to just 20% in January.

Ben Nevis is arguably the best winter climbing centre in the country. Its altitude and topography ensure a wintry condition from December through to mid-April, although a proximity to the coast makes it vulnerable to thaw conditions — and the inevitable devastating avalanches — induced by mild south-westerly winds. Protection on the harder winter climbs is frequently poor. The few cracks and spikes are often obscured, placing a heavy reliance on snow or ice anchors. However, with cunning, it is possible to safeguard most routes using modern protection equipment.

June and July are probably the best months for rock climbing. Earlier than this, the remnants of winter snow could be a serious inconvenience, while in later months the weather becomes more unsettled. The rock is a volcanic type known as andesite, which is of a dark, sombre appearance for the most part, but slightly reddish in areas when very dry. The quality varies from indifferent to excellent. On Ben Nevis will be found the longest, most sustained climbs on good rock in the country.

Approaches: Ben Nevis (GR:167 713) lies 7km south-east of Fort William. The main A82 road between Glasgow and Inverness passes through the town, which is also served by rail. There are no seasonal access restrictions.

Approaches to CIC Hut

1. **From Achintee:** This is the best summer approach. In winter the Meall an t-Suidhe section is exposed to wind, while the contouring section can be difficult to find and follow. Start from Achintee at GR:124 730. Alternatively, start from the Youth Hostel in Glen Nevis, joining the main path after about 1km. The tourist path leads in about 2.5km to the bealach between Meall an t-Suidhe and Carn Dearg. Continue north-north-east, along a comparatively level but sometimes muddy path, to gain the north

edge of the bealach (cairn). The path now descends to the right for about 50m, before contouring north-east under the north face of Carn Dearg. Eventually it leads to the CIC Hut at an altitude of 680m. 2hrs 30mins.

2. **From the Golf Course:**   This is the best winter approach. Start from the private golf course at GR:136 763, 2km north of Fort William on the A82 (use discretion when parking here). Walk under the railway line, and follow a track and path over the golf course (the path is marked on OS Sheet 41). Cross the deer fence, and continue by the obvious, and occasionally very boggy, uphill path to reach the forestry road at the dam. (Note that the gates on the forestry road are normally locked, although a key may be hired from the local Forestry Office. It begins at Torlundy, 1km north of the golf course, but savings on time and energy are questionable — the road surface is poor, and your vehicle may become trapped by a heavy snowfall.) Above the dam, the path ascends steadily through bogs to the CIC Hut; easy to follow in daylight, much less so at night. 2hrs.

Accommodation: Hotels and other accommodation in Fort William, plus the usual urban amenities, most of which remain open throughout the winter. Youth Hostel and nearby campsite in Glen Nevis (GR:127 717), both of which are convenient for the tourist path up Ben Nevis. Wild camping further up Glen Nevis, and in the Allt a'Mhuilinn glen (poor sites, especially in winter). The SMC's Charles Inglis Clark (CIC) Memorial Hut is ideally placed under the cliffs at an altitude of 680m (GR:166 723). Such is the demand for winter bedspace here that bookings (via your club secretary) must be made one year in advance, and then with no guarantee of success. However, it may be possible to secure a well-advanced booking for a summer visit.

DESCENTS

Only careful navigation will extricate you from the summit plateau in poor visibility (map and compass essential).

1.   **Via the Red Burn and Tourist Path to Achintee:**   Simple to follow in good visibility, notoriously difficult in bad. A common error is to veer too soon towards Glen Nevis. In winter, therefore, consider descending initially to the top of No.4 Gully — as for 3 — to be certain of locating the Red Burn.

2.   **Via the Carn Mor Dearg Arete and Abseil Posts to CIC Hut:**   With care, this can make a better winter descent in bad visibility than 3. However, avoid if the initial slope is icy. Do not attempt a direct descent from the summit shelter to the top of the abseil posts — the Little Brenva Face intervenes. Instead, follow a bearing of about 135 degrees magnetic for approximately 400m (occasional marker poles). Now trend east to locate the first abseil post on the arete, which here is almost level. There is nothing to be gained by abseiling. Instead, zigzag down the slope in the vicinity of the posts to enter Coire Leis.

3.   **Via No.4 Gully and Coire na Ciste to CIC Hut:**   This is the most popular descent to the hut. However, extra time spent on the plateau in bad weather prolongs exposure to wind and magnifies the risk of route-finding error (but resist the temptation to cut short and descend Tower Gully — it is liable to avalanche and is undercut by hidden cliffs). Confirm progress by identifying major landmarks on the plateau edge (refer to sketch map opposite). The shallow col at the top of No.4 Gully is marked by a pole and metal flag. A descent of No.4 Gully is almost always possible (if not, descend the Red Burn to the tourist track and contour back to the CIC Hut via the Achintee approach path). The top 20m or so are the steepest. If necessary, the pole can provide a belay while cutting a slot in the cornice (but don't expect to be able to abseil over *and* retrieve the ropes!). The precise descent from Coire na Ciste to the CIC Hut depends on conditions.

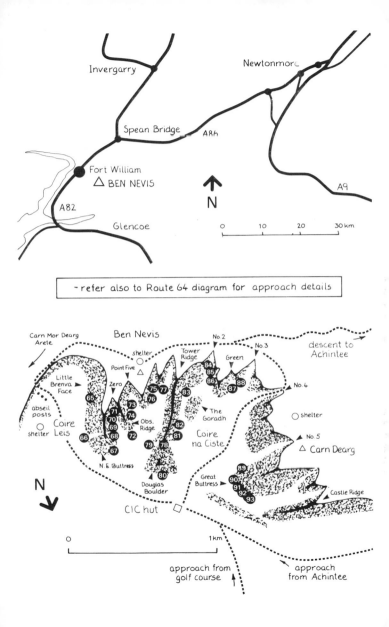

Invergarry

Newtonmore

Spean Bridge

A86

Fort William
△ BEN NEVIS

A82

Glencoe

A9

N

0   10   20   30 km

- refer also to Route 64 diagram for approach details

Carn Mor Dearg Arete

Ben Nevis

No. 2

No. 3

descent to Achintee

shelter

Point Five

Tower Ridge

Green

84
85
86
87
88

Little Brenva Face

Zero

75 77
76

83

No. 4

65

71
73

The Garadh

abseil posts

70
69

74

shelter

82

66

Coire Leis

68

72

79 78

81

Coire na Ciste

No. 5
△ Carn Dearg

shelter

67

N. E. Buttress

80

89
90
91
92
93

N

Douglas Boulder

Great Buttress

Castle Ridge

CIC hut

0   1 km

approach from golf course

approach from Achintee

Alastair Walker on the final arete of Minus One direct (Route 69),
Ben Nevis. (Photo: Ken Crocket)

Tony Ashton on the 'sinister gully' of Observatory Ridge (Route 72), Ben Nevis. (Photo: Steve Ashton)

Ken Crocket starting the Eastern Traverse on Tower Ridge (Route 79), Ben Nevis. (Photo: Crocket Collection)

Looking down Glover's Chimney (Route 83), Ben Nevis. (Photo: Steve Ashton)

64: CARN MOR DEARG ARETE (E) 18km

Summary: A grand hill-walking traverse, incorporating the summits of Carn Mor Dearg and Ben Nevis. The linking arete is exposed but straightforward. Views of the vast and complex cliffs on the north face of Ben Nevis are stunning.

First Ascent: Not known.

Best Conditions: Early summer is probably the best time (May to July). If much snow persists, crampons and ice-axe should be carried.

Approach: As described, the route begins and ends at Achintee Farm, at the start of the Ben Nevis tourist path. Leave Fort William on the A82 heading north, cross the Nevis Bridge, and take the minor road on the right leading in 2km to Achintee (parking space). It is also possible to start from the Youth Hostel in Glen Nevis, joining the main path after about 1km.

Starting Point: Achintee Farm (GR: 124 730).

Descent: See below.

The well-maintained tourist path leads in about 2.5km to the grassy bealach between Meall an t-Suidhe and Carn Dearg. From here a reasonably level path heads north-north-east to gain the north edge of the bealach. Rough, heathery slopes lead down to the Allt a'Mhuilinn (difficult crossing in spate). The summit of Carn Beag Dearg (1010m) is gained after a 600m ascent to the east up bouldery slopes.

Views of the cliffs opposite are outstanding, with the dark bulk of Carn Dearg Buttress prominent. The ridge now leads airily in 2km over Carn Dearg Meadhonach (1179m) to gain the summit of Carn Mor Dearg (1223m). With this progress the subtle shift in viewpoint increasingly emphasises Tower Ridge and the vast North-East Buttress, which gains stature with every step.

From the summit, the ridge drops to the south, gradually swings south-west, and, after 200m of descent, narrows into a granite arete. Its crest gives an exposed scramble, but this should not present any difficulties (though greasy when wet). If necessary it can be avoided by a parallel path on the Glen Nevis (south-east) flank. The views to the Grey Coires, and east to the Aonachs, are particularly impressive.

A short distance before the ridge rears up to give the final climb to Ben Nevis, an abseil post on the rim of the coire marks a line of descent northwards into Coire Leis (uncomplicated scree unless covered in snow). A party facing darkness or bad weather might use this as an escape route into the Allt a'Mhuilinn Glen. Otherwise, boulders lead steeply to the summit of Ben Nevis (stay clear of the cliff edge on the right during this

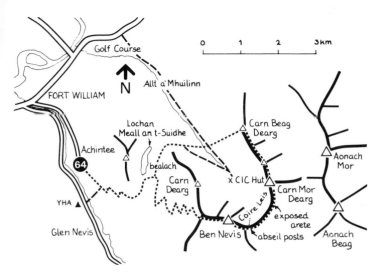

ascent, and instead follow the faint path among boulders). If the day is clear, your arrival on the summit will be rewarded by a vast panorama of hills, sea, and lochs. If not, interest will be confined to the trig. point on its cairn, and the nearby emergency shelter built on the ruins of the meteorological observatory.

Be careful to avoid the cliff edges while on the summit area, particularly if snow is present (when you may inadvertently wander on to the unsupported lips of overhanging cornices). Stones dislodged from the cliff tops will also endanger climbers down below.

The descent path is well marked, and leads down the broad back of the mountain, rejoining the ascent path at the Glen Nevis end of the bealach between Meall an t'Suidhe and Carn Dearg.

65: CRESTA CLIMB (III) 300m

Summary: A splendid introduction to Ben Nevis face climbing.
Mostly snow, but may include
several ice pitches. The headwall
provides a cliff-hanging finale!
Deadmen, ice screws and rock
pegs required for belays.

First Ascent: T.W. Patey, L.S.
Lovat and A.G. Nicol, February
1957.

Best Conditions: Conditions are
very variable on this face because
of its exposure to sunlight. After
snowfall, it may consolidate quickly
and become icy, or it may simply
continue thawing until stripped.
After New Year is usually the best
period.

Approach: Refer to area
introduction for approaches to the
CIC Hut. Continue up the path
parallel to the Allt a'Mhuilinn,
passing the lowest rocks of the
North-East Buttress, to enter Coire
Leis. The Little Brenva Face rises
from the right-hand side of the inner
coire. Identify the route before
approaching too closely. 45mins
(plus hut approach time).

Starting Point: In a snow bay,
roughly central to the line of cliffs.
This can be difficult to locate even
in clear weather (use diagrams to
help identify features), and virtually
impossible in mist.

Descent: Refer to descent notes
in the area introduction.

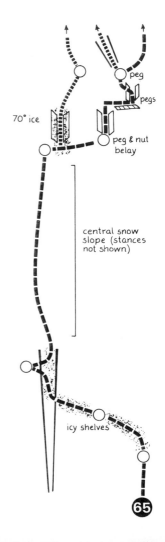

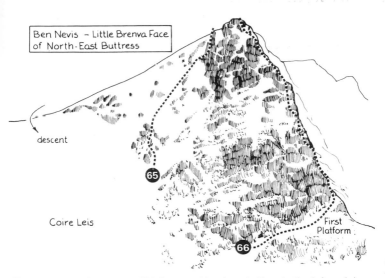

Ben Nevis – Little Brenva Face
of North-East Buttress

descent

Coire Leis

First
Platform

From the snow bay, you will follow a raking ice shelf up to the left, gaining a small gully in two pitches. After climbing the gully, you will simply follow the most natural line up the open face. There is no precise line. If these slopes seem interminable, spare a thought for the step-cutting trio on the first ascent; two wore nailed boots, while the third wore vibrams without crampons!

The headwall appears to bar an exit to the plateau. A steep (70 degree) ice pitch offers the best hope, particularly as it soon leads to easy slopes. But why not follow the pioneers? First, traverse right for about 30m to reach a steep corner (peg and nut belay). Now climb the corner to a shelf, which leads rightwards into a rock corner under a buttress wall. Ascend steeply now for a few moves (look out for old peg runners), until it is possible to step back left and move up to a small outcrop and peg belay. An interesting, varied and crucial pitch! Finally, climb mixed ground on the right. Alternatively, if time is pressing, go left and climb an easy snow gully to the plateau rim.

66: NORTH-EAST BUTTRESS (III) 500m +

Summary: One of the three great Ben Nevis ridges. A magnificent but serious expedition, with major difficulties high on the route. 'Interesting' route-finding. Good belays throughout, mostly on rock.

First Ascent: Winter − W.W. Naismith, W. Brunskill, A.B.W. Kennedy, W.W. King and F.C. Squance, April 1896.

Best Conditions: Climbable under most conditions, although chimney and corner pitches benefit from firm snow. Ascents after mid-February enjoy valuable extra daylight.

Approach: Refer to area introduction for approaches to the CIC Hut. Continue up the path parallel to the Allt a'Mhuilinn, passing to the left of the lowest rocks of the North-East Buttress. 45mins (plus hut approach time).

Starting Point: Start where a large sloping shelf leads rightwards on to the shoulder of the First Platform.

Descent: Refer to descent notes in the area introduction.

This great ridge had been first climbed in the summer of 1892 by the Hopkinson family from Manchester, who modestly reported their ascent in the *Alpine Journal*. The prospect of a first winter ascent mobilised the SMC stalwarts, who in 1896 held their second Fort William Easter Meet. Thus did a large party from the Alexandria Hotel make their slow way up the buttress − although their time of seven hours is still respectable, for a large party with short ropes.

Snow conditions, and hence difficulties, are very variable on the shelf traverse to the First Platform. Above, the ridge narrows spectacularly. Where it steepens, a devious rightward traverse leads to a chimney line. This slants left to regain the crest at the indistinct Second Platform. There now follows an interlude of sustained, but mostly straightforward, climbing.

The Mantrap interrupts the flow. This little nose of rock, barely 3m high, is a formidable obstacle. An *in situ* peg, or combined tactics, may assist a strenuous pull-up. If these antics are unsuccessful, there are two alternatives − a slabby corner on the right (dependent on good snow), or a short, overhanging wall on the left (the original mantrap). One more difficult pitch remains − the Forty-Foot Corner. Formed by two slabby walls, it will be climbed direct or not at all. When inadequately iced it can be turned, though not without difficulty, on the left.

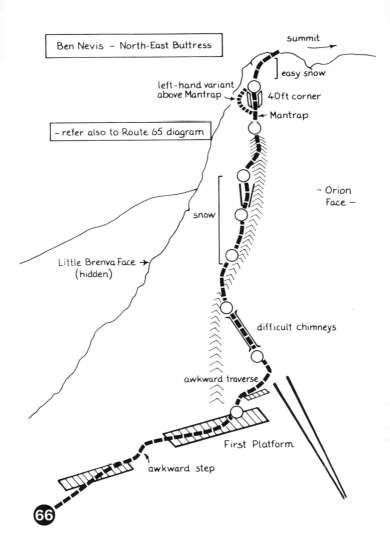

Ben Nevis - North-East Buttress

summit →

easy snow

left-hand variant
above Mantrap →

40ft corner

← Mantrap

- refer also to Route 65 diagram

- Orion
Face -

snow

Little Brenva Face →
(hidden)

difficult chimneys

awkward traverse

First Platform

awkward step

66

67: RAEBURN'S ARETE (S) 225m

Summary: One of the cleanest and steepest *Severes* on Ben Nevis. Climbs superb, rough andesite in good position. Deserves to be better known.

First Ascent: H. Raeburn, Dr and Mrs Inglis Clark, June 1902.

Best Conditions: Requires about two midsummer days to dry out after rain (allow an extra day in colder weather). Usually climbable between May and October.

Approach: Refer to area introduction for approaches to the CIC Hut. The North-East Buttress will be seen directly ahead. The grassy shelf on top of a supporting buttress is the First Platform. Above the hut, follow the path which approximately parallels the burn to reach the buttress. 45mins (plus hut approach time).

Starting Point: The North and East Faces of the buttress meet at an arete. Start at the lowest rocks beneath the arete.

Descent: (1) Via Raeburn's 18-Minute Route (*M*), which forms the left (north) wall of Slingsby's Chimney (the gully between the First Platform and the main mass of the North-East Buttress). This requires care. Go down a series of short walls, traverses, and corners, parallel to Slingsby's Chimney.

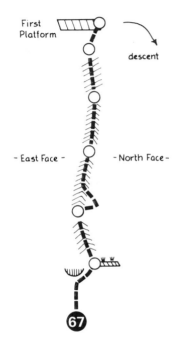

From about half-way down the buttress, cross into Slingsby's Chimney, and descend via loose rocks to the screes. These lead across into Observatory Gully, which in turn leads easily to below the start; or (2) from the First Platform, traverse down and left along a broken shelf leading to Coire Leis.

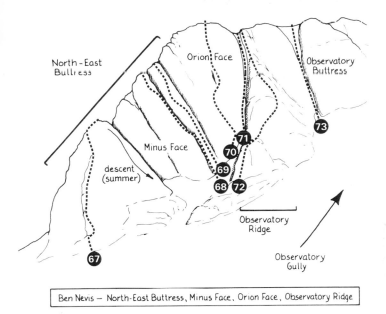

North-East
Buttress

Orion Face

Observatory
Buttress

Minus Face

descent
(summer)

Observatory
Ridge

Observatory
Gully

67 68 69 70 71 72 73

Ben Nevis — North-East Buttress, Minus Face, Orion Face, Observatory Ridge

By 1902, Raeburn was much the best rock climber in Scotland (fifteen of the thirty first ascents recorded on Ben Nevis between 1896 and 1921 were his). In a June heat wave, he joined the Clarks for a week's climbing based at the summit 'hotel'. An active week of exploration climaxed with this route, which Raeburn considered would have been impossible but for the magnificent nature of the rock.

Above the start lies a black overhang, passed on the right to a ledge and belay. A pitch up the arete is followed by a 6m rightward traverse, after which the arete is regained and followed to the top. The rock and situations are excellent, with a continuing view down the Glen, and superb cliff panoramas to the right.

68: MINUS TWO GULLY (V) 275m

Summary: A sustained ice climb,
linking a series of chimneys and
grooves to give one of the best of
Ben Nevis gullies. Medium-sized
Friends useful in addition to the
usual protection equipment.

First Ascent: J.R. Marshall, J.
Stenhouse and D. Haston, February
1959.

Best Conditions: Conditions on
the Minus Face are quirky and
unpredictable. Lack of drainage
means that heavy snow followed by
a period of freeze-thaw produces
the best material. January and
February might offer the best
chance of an ascent.

Approach: Refer to area introduction for approaches to CIC Hut.
Continue   towards   North-East
Buttress, entering the wide mouth
of Observatory Gully (beware
avalanche   conditions).   Cross
directly towards the gully. 45mins
(plus hut approach time).

Starting Point: At the foot of the
gully (refer to Route 67 diagram).

Descent: Refer to descent notes
in the area introduction. Alternatively, if time is short or conditions
bad, abseil to the First Platform
(two long, one short), and descend
eastwards across the large, sloping
shelf to easy ground in Coire Leis.
Some knowledge of the buttress is
recommended before attempting
this descent.

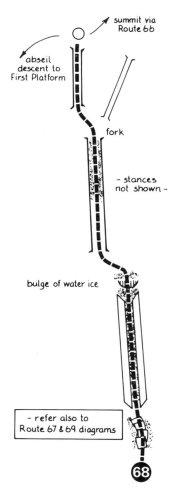

Of the four great Ben Nevis gullies — Zero, Point Five, Minus One, and Minus Two — it is Minus Two which gives the most interesting and varied climbing. It includes icy grooves and slabs, an ice bulge at a fork in the gully, and a chimney exit to North East Buttress. As if that wasn't enough, there is still the Mantrap and Forty-Foot Corner to be negotiated before the climb is finished.

Minus Two is in condition much less often than the big face climbs, or the pure snow and ice gullies of Zero and Point Five, but it is well worth the wait.

The first ascent involved step-cutting. Dougal Haston, later of Everest fame, commented that it took as long to second the pitches as it did for Marshall to lead them — a vivid reminder of Marshall's skill.

The first pitch is a good indicator of what will follow, as the leader steps straight on to steep snow in a corner. Depending on build-up, it should be possible to climb this more or less directly to gain a bulging rib of ice above. The angle of the rib is not too severe — perhaps 70 degrees — although it may be thinly coated.

More sustained climbing follows in the grooves above, until a short leftwards traverse leads to the main chimney of the climb. This should present few problems, except for a bulge of water-ice which may force a strenuous traverse on dinner-plating ice, bombarding the second with debris. Ice screws will be of little use here, adding to the second's anxiety.

To a tired party, the finishing chimneys look formidable. But in good snow they turn out to be friendly enough, with the reassurance of a solid rock wall against which to rest one's back. The crest of the buttress arrives suddenly, its huge block belays welcome after the scarcity of flakes and cracks in the gully. But hold back the celebrations for a little while — the crux of the North-East Buttress is yet to come.

69: MINUS ONE DIRECT (HVS) 260m

Summary: Ascends a slender buttress in an Alpine environment. Perhaps the best route at this grade in the country. Sustained.

First Ascent: Original line — R.O. Downes, M.J. O'Hara and M. Prestige, June 1956. Serendipity Variation — K.V. Crocket and I. Fulton, August 1972.

Best Conditions: Requires 2 or 3 days to dry after rain. Usually climbable between May and October, depending on snow conditions.

Approach: Refer to area introduction for approaches to CIC Hut. Continue towards North-East Buttress to the foot of Observatory

Gully, then ascend easy rocks below Observatory Ridge to enter the basin on the left, below Zero Gully (caution with bergschrunds here). 45mins (plus hut approach time).

Starting Point: Below the lowest rocks of the buttress, beneath a corner.

Descent: Descend the ridge of North-East Buttress to the Second Platform (a sloping shelf on the ridge crest). Now go down short chimneys and grooves, a shallow gully, and a narrow ridge, on to the First Platform. Finally, descend Raeburn's 18-Minute Route to the foot of the face, as for Route 67.

The precise length of the first pitch depends on the depth of snow at its foot. In any event, a corner leads to a belay on the right. A difficult move up a shallow groove on the left wall begins the second pitch, which continues via a block — climbed by a crack on its right — and walls to a niche on the left.

The third pitch takes the pillar on the right without difficulty, while the fourth contains the original crux — an undercut groove found above an undercut nose, and at the right end of a ledge. Delicate and committing moves up the groove win a block belay up on the right.

The wide crack above leads into a poor section of Minus One Gully, so traverse left to an edge on the superior Serendipity Variation (so called because it was climbed by chance), and gain a slab by a difficult move. The slab and grooves above lead in two pitches to a large terrace and huge flake on the original route. The flake, ridge crest, and shattered horizontal arete beyond, lead on to the North-East Buttress.

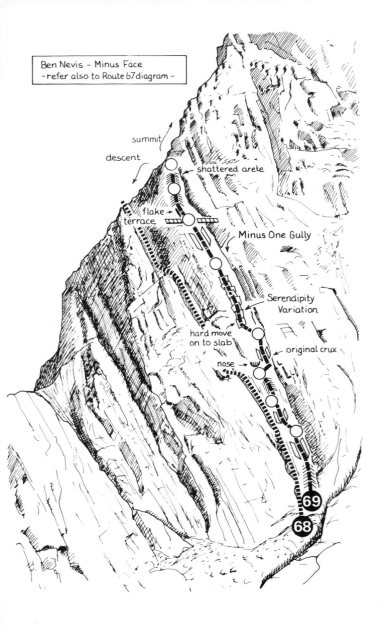

Ben Nevis - Minus Face
- refer also to Route 67 diagram -

summit

descent

shattered arete

flake
terrace

Minus One Gully

Serendipity
Variation

hard move
on to slab

original crux

nose

69
68

70: ORION FACE DIRECT (V) 400m

Summary: A magnificent face climb of Alpine proportions — long, sustained and serious. Technical difficulties are not excessive in good conditions. Adequate protection when the ice is sufficiently thick, otherwise expect several poor belays. Demands careful route-finding.

First Ascent: J.R. Marshall and R. Smith, February 1960.

Best Conditions: Avoid powder snow and thin ice. Best period: February to April.

Approach: Refer to area introduction for approaches to CIC Hut. Continue towards North-East Buttress, entering the wide mouth of Observatory Gully (beware avalanche conditions). Refer to Route 67 diagram, and enter the snowfield below Zero Gully. 1hr (plus hut approach time).

Starting Point: Below and to the left of Zero Gully, where an iced slab leads to the foot of a corner (the corner runs up the left side of a small buttress).

Descent: Refer to descent notes in area introduction.

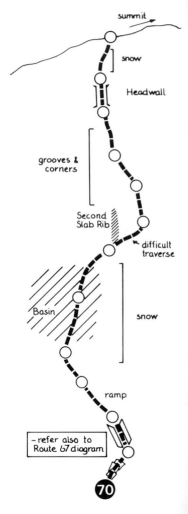

summit

snow

Headwall

grooves & corners

Second Slab Rib

difficult traverse

Basin

snow

ramp

– refer also to Route 67 diagram

70

The first pitch leads easily up to the right, on an iced slab, to a belay at the foot of an obvious corner. Here, excavation may reveal one of the few good rock belays on the climb. The second pitch is the first of three key pitches. It climbs the steep, icy corner to a belay below a roof. The way seems barred, but a leftward traverse, followed by easing ground up to the right, leads in two pitches to the Basin — the snow-filled hollow in the middle of the face.

The aim now is to gain the foot of the Second Slab Rib at the top right-hand side of the Basin (the Rib is often seen from the approach as an isolated dark strip). The second good belay on the route may be found at the foot of the rib, where a peg and nut on its edge protect the second key pitch — the Traverse. Thus secured, swing out right and gingerly step across sloping ledges, hoping to find solid ice or snow. With luck you might discover a rounded spike to provide additional protection for this section. Better holds appear near the end of the traverse, and a ledge above the wall provides a stance — if not a belay. A well-balanced partnership is important on this route! From this airy stance you can look down on Observatory Ridge, although the steep pitches of Zero Gully will be hidden by bulges of ice.

Several excellent pitches now lead up to the left, over switch-back grooves and walls of ice, to a small snow basin under the headwall. Here you will move slightly left to a good belay under a narrow chimney — the third key pitch. The second, strapped to a good peg in the horizontal crack, may well feel awed by the atmosphere of this giant face while the leader fights it out in the steep chimney above — especially if twilight's last gleam is creeping over the mountain. But the desperate-looking roof above is avoided by a short, rightward traverse. And after that just a few moves will secure your admittance to that select band who have climbed the Orion Face Direct.

71: ZERO GULLY (IV/V) 300m

Summary: One of the classic Ben Nevis gullies. Ice pitches angled at $70-80+$ degrees in the initial section are followed by short pitches and straightforward snow bashing. Belays are normally on ice or snow, so deadmen and a good selection of screws and drive-ins are required.

First Ascent: H. MacInnes, A.G. Nicol and T.W. Patey, February 1957.

Best Conditions: Avoid after snowfall or when powder snow is prevalent, as the gully is very prone to avalanche and spindrift. The colour of the first pitch is a useful indicator — grey means the climb will be thin and hard, whereas white means there is sufficient material for a standard ascent (provided it is of the appropriate consistency). February and March are usually the best months.

Approach: As for Route 70.

Starting Point: At the foot of the gully, between Orion Face and Observatory Ridge.

Descent: Refer to descent notes in area introduction.

This route has long been famous, its notoriety built on the epic history of attempts by the leading climbers of the day. Since then, due to the scourge of front-pointing, it has suffered a demotion in technical difficulty. Nevertheless, because of belaying difficulties and avalanche risks, its reputation for seriousness is undiminished.

The major technical difficulties will all be found in the first 100m or so. Normally a shallow trough or groove will be found rising slightly left of the true gully bed towards rock overhangs. This will give one long and one short pitch, of about 70 and 80 degrees respectively. The second of these leads up to a rock belay (often buried), from where a difficult rightward traverse, across a bulging wall, re-enters the main gully line. Those who thought all this section looked too easy would have climbed directly to this point up a bulging ice rib on the right of the normal start.

Difficulties gradually ease above, although there may be one awkward ice wall, and several minor ice pitches, before the gully falls back as an unbroken snow-filled trough. It drags interminably when sunlight beckons on the plateau rim.

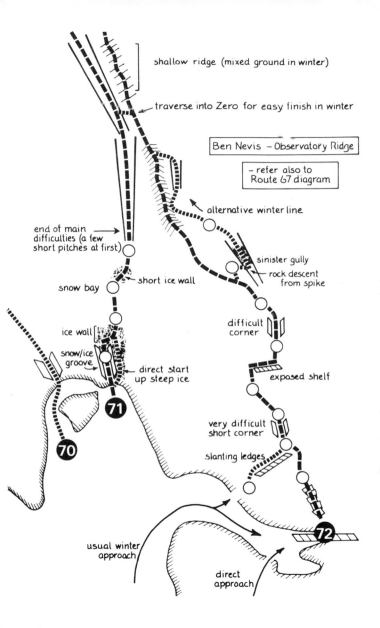

shallow ridge (mixed ground in winter)

traverse into Zero for easy finish in winter

Ben Nevis – Observatory Ridge

– refer also to
Route 67 diagram

alternative winter line

end of main
difficulties (a few
short pitches at first)

sinister gully
rock descent
from spike

short ice wall

snow bay

difficult
corner

ice wall

exposed shelf

snow/ice
groove

direct start
up steep ice

71

very difficult
short corner

70

slanting ledges

72

usual winter
approach

direct
approach

72: OBSERVATORY RIDGE (D+) 420m

Summary: A ridge of alpine character set amid the most impressive cliff architecture in Britain. Very much a mountain-eering route, particularly when complicated by old snow in the upper reaches. Difficulties are mostly confined to the lower section, where several moves approach *V. Diff* standard. (Illustrated on Route 71 diagram.)

First Ascent: H. Raeburn, June 1901.

Best Conditions: Allow 2 days

to dry. Usually climbable from late May to October, although snow patches in the upper regions may linger until July.

Approach: As for Route 69 to the foot of the ridge. 45mins (plus hut approach time).

Starting Point: At the lowest rocks of the ridge, below the right end of an obvious ledge seen from the approach.

Descent: Refer to descent notes in area introduction.

The name of Harold Raeburn is inextricably linked to this climb, as he made both the first summer ascent (solo), and in 1921 the first winter ascent.

In June 1901, Raeburn went up Nevis to meet his friends, the Clarks. Arriving without a partner, he walked through a cloudburst to climb the ridge. After the ascent he recalled three good sections to the climb; the slabby rocks near the foot, a hand traverse above the ledge, and a steep tower at over half-height, which he turned on the right. His ascent took three hours.

Slabby rocks at the foot lead in two pitches to the right end of the large ledge. The line continues just left of the crest until steep rocks force a traverse right, leading to a corner system with cracks and grooves. These access the easier-angled rocks above, which are followed with little difficulty to the summit. The views across Observatory Gully and to the huge Orion and Minus Faces are breathtaking.

Crampon scratches show the way, should there be any doubt as to the line of the route (most difficulties are turned on the right). In keeping with its alpine nature, speed of movement is important, particularly after a late start.

OBSERVATORY RIDGE IN WINTER (III/IV) 400m +

Summary: The most difficult of the three classic ridges on the mountain. Front-pointing has made little impact on the inherent difficulties of this route. Consider carefully all parameters before making an attempt. Belays are good (mostly rock), although some pitches are poorly protected. (Illustrated on Route 71 diagram.)

First Ascent: H. Raeburn, F.S. Goggs and W.A. Mounsey, April 1920.

Best Conditions: Hard going in anything other than a good cover of firm snow. Knowledge of the route in summer will be of immense value in finding the best line, otherwise follow the scratches. An ascent late in the season benefits from extra daylight.

Approach: As for Route 70 to the snow slope below Zero Gully. Purists will climb the initial section of ridge, as for the summer route, while the impatient will ascend the snow slope below Zero and then traverse rightwards on to the obvious snow shelf. 45mins (plus hut approach time).

Starting Point: On the snow shelf, either at the foot of parallel breaks which slant up to the right (just before the shelf dips steeply down to the right), or below the ridge crest at its lower right end.

Descent: Refer to descent notes in area introduction.

There are two ways to leave the snow shelf — by the parallel breaks or, using the lower starting point, by the blunt ridge crest. Both lead to the foot of a corner crack. Summer or winter, this provides an obstinate problem, as the scratches on the rock will testify. A pessimist would remind you that one abseil from here returns you to the starting shelf! Fortunately, the belay is excellent. An odd mixture of brute force and balance climbing seems to get results, although you might like to place a Friend for protection in case it doesn't.

There are many more difficult pitches above, particularly where a step on the ridge is turned on the right by a gloomy, ice-filled gutter. Eventually the ridge falls back into a succession of snow crests, gullies, and baffling walls. If snow conditions allow, a great deal of time will be saved by moving left to finish by the easy upper part of Zero Gully.

73: POINT FIVE GULLY (V) 300m

Summary: The longest and most difficult of the mountain's pure snow and ice gullies. Major difficulties are concentrated in the first 100m, although the upper gully includes several minor ice pitches. Technically more difficult than Zero, but better protected. Carry a good selection of screws and drive-ins, a few rock pegs, plus deadmen for the upper section.

First Ascent: J.M. Alexander, I.S. Clough, D. Pipes and R. Shaw, January 1959.

Best Conditions: Frequently in condition, although obviously more difficult during lean periods in early and late season. Crowds are a serious problem during weekends and holiday periods. Avoid times of heavy snow.

Approach: Refer to area introduction for approaches to CIC Hut. Now go up under the Douglas Boulder, entering Observatory Gully (beware avalanche conditions). Trend left from about half-way up the gully, entering the recess between Observatory Ridge on the left, and Observatory Buttress on the right. 45mins (plus hut approach time).

Starting Point: At the foot of the gully.

Descent: Refer to descent notes in area introduction.

Many early attempts on Point Five were foiled by the powder snow avalanches which regularly funnel into the confines of the gully. Other attempts failed, disastrously, because of hopelessly inadequate ice-axe belays. The eventual first ascent proved to be a highly controversial affair — the siege involved 40 hours of gully work spread over a period of 6 days. Bolts from this ascent may still be found on the route, though only in lean conditions.

In normal conditions, a slabby barrel of a first pitch leads to a stance under a wall. The ice-choked groove now rears up. It will give some very steep climbing before lying back into a fine little bowl.

The third pitch (or fourth, if the previous long pitch was split) is shaped somewhat like a bottle. The angle at its neck approaches vertical, and many consider it to be the crux. The gully saves its most prolonged powder avalanche until you are committed on this final bulge! Seemingly endless pitches above are an anticlimax, but nothing will detract from that special moment as you pull over the cornice on to the summit plateau.

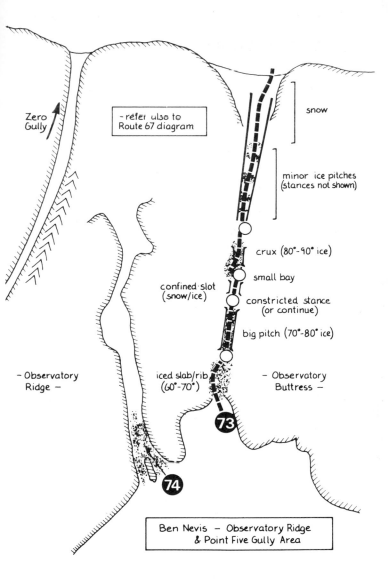

Zero Gully

refer also to Route 67 diagram

snow

minor ice pitches (stances not shown)

crux (80°-90° ice)

small bay

constricted stance (or continue)

big pitch (70°-80° ice)

confined slot (snow/ice)

iced slab/rib (60°-70°)

— Observatory Ridge —

— Observatory Buttress —

73

74

Ben Nevis — Observatory Ridge & Point Five Gully Area

74: HADRIAN'S WALL DIRECT (V) 300m

Summary: A scenic route, with excellent ice climbing. In some ways a shorter version of the Orion Face. Steep ice leads to a snow section, followed by (optional) mixed climbing on the upper buttress. Often in condition. Carry deadmen in addition to a good selection of ice protection.

First Ascent: M.G. Geddes and G. Little, April 1971.

Best Conditions: The prominent ice-fall of the route is easily visible from the approach, and when in good condition will appear complete. The route generally builds up from late December onwards. Avoid during avalanche conditions, when loose snow may funnel down the chimney pitch.

Approach: As for Route 73. 45mins (plus hut approach time).

Starting Point: Below the right-hand side of the prominent ice-fall, about 60m or so down to the left from the foot of Point Five Gully.

Descent: Refer to descent notes in area introduction.

The first section − a gradually steepening scoop − is an ice climber's delight. It ends at a short rock wall where, unless the ice is very thick, you should find a rock belay. Otherwise resort to a cut step and ice screws − with the usual feelings of trepidation this brings.

From the stance, the leader will move slightly right before going up to break over the steepest part of the route − a near-vertical wall of ice. Above is a snow shelf, at the top right of which is a short chimney. This leads to the large snow basin, from which there is a choice of routes. The usual line continues more or less directly above, finishing up a fine corner to the right of Observatory Ridge. It is also possible to move left on to Observatory Ridge itself, with its optional fast finish on the upper section of Zero Gully. But if time and fitness allow, why not move right on to the upper wall? This provides a far more appropriate finish, as the route meanders through grooves and walls in a series of sustained pitches.

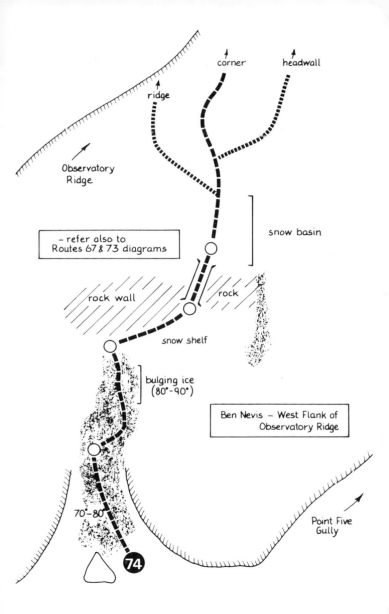

corner

headwall

ridge

Observatory
Ridge

snow basin

– refer also to
Routes 67 & 73 diagrams

rock wall

rock

snow shelf

bulging ice
(80°–90°)

Ben Nevis – West Flank of
Observatory Ridge

70–80

74

Point Five
Gully

75: GARDYLOO GULLY (II/III) 150m

Summary: A useful and interesting route in the sparse conditions of early season (when it may be a grade harder). Rock features may all but bank out later in the season. Includes one difficult pitch in average conditions. Deadmen essential.

First Ascent: G. Hastings and W.P. Haskett-Smith, April 1897.

Best Conditions: Climbable at almost any time of the season, except when avalanche conditions prevail (the approach is especially vulnerable). The difficulty of the crux will vary greatly according to the quantity of snow. In exceptional conditions, there may be a cornice finish.

Approach: Refer to area introduction for approaches to CIC Hut. From the hut, ascend below the Douglas Boulder and enter Observatory Gully (which is really a broad couloir). It does not in itself extend to the summit plateau, but splits into two branches on either side of Gardyloo Buttress — Tower Gully on the right, and Gardyloo Gully on the left. Ascend the couloir to its top left-hand side. 1hr (plus hut approach time).

Starting Point: At the foot of the obvious deep gully.

Descent: Refer to descent notes in area introduction.

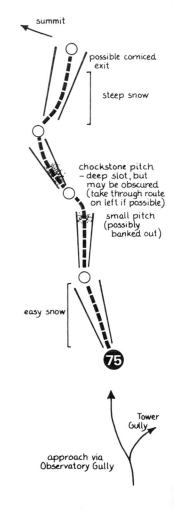

summit

possible corniced exit

steep snow

chockstone pitch – deep slot, but may be obscured (take through route on left if possible)

small pitch (possibly banked out)

easy snow

75

Tower Gully

approach via Observatory Gully

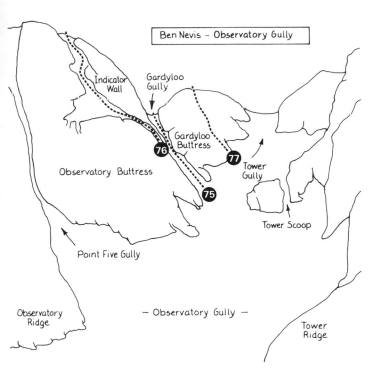

Ben Nevis - Observatory Gully

Indicator Wall

Gardyloo Gully

Gardyloo Buttress

76

77

Tower Gully

Observatory Buttress

75

Tower Scoop

Point Five Gully

Observatory Ridge

— Observatory Gully —

Tower Ridge

In 1897, the SMC did not hold their Easter Meet at Fort William (as in the previous year), but at Tyndrum. They must have been more than a little peeved, therefore, to learn that a group from the Alpine Club had been up to Ben Nevis and had 'poached' several routes, including Tower Gully and Gardyloo Gully.

The ascent of Tower Gully (*l*) had been witnessed by the four staff members of the summit Meteorological Observatory, where the climbers were later welcomed with a meal. The following day, two of the successful Tower Gully party succeeded on Gardyloo Gully. This must have been a somewhat messy outing — the gully was used by Observatory staff as a rubbish tip!

76: GOOD FRIDAY CLIMB (III) 150m

Summary: An impressive route which finds an unlikely breach in the highest crag in the country. Four or five varied pitches lead through interesting scenery to a choice of finishes. The crux can be protected. Carry deadmen and rock pegs in addition to other protection gear.

First Ascent: G.G. Macphee, R.W. Lovell, H.R. Shepherd and D. Edwards, April 1939.

Best Conditions: Normally in condition from New Year onwards. Avoid after heavy snowfall, and during thaw.

Approach: As for Route 75, then traverse left along an easy but exposed terrace. Some parties may wish to rope-up for this traverse, particularly as there is a substantial cliff beneath. Be watchful of snow conditions throughout this approach. 1hr (plus hut approach time).

Starting Point: On the snow terrace, at the foot of an obvious gully (or at the start of the terrace traverse, depending on conditions).

Descent: Refer to descent notes in area introduction.

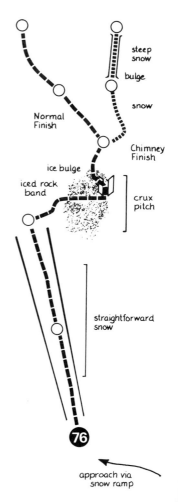

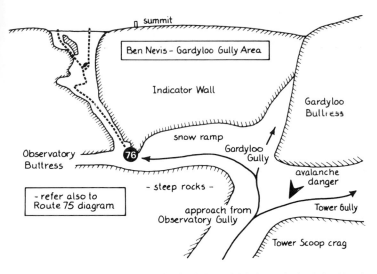

This high-altitude route climbs the fault line which bounds the left side of Indicator Wall, so named because of the viewpoint indicator built above its slabby face next to the summit. The indicator was vandalised in the 1940s. Nothing changes.

The initial gully leads in two pitches to a cul-de-sac, where, with a little searching, a belay may be found for the next, crucial pitch. This begins with a step out right on to a ledge, followed by a few rightward moves to gain a short corner. You might find an old peg in the niche at its top. This, or an alternative runner, will protect a swing out left on to the ice boss. Easy ground above the pull-up leads to a small rock outcrop, where a good spike awaits excavation.

There is a choice of finishes. The normal route goes up to the left, whereas the chimney finish follows Indicator Wall up a fine corner on the right. Either finish leads in two pitches to the summit cairn, around which a sling may be conveniently dropped to secure the highest belay in the land.

77: SMITH'S ROUTE (V) 130m

Summary: A high-angled ice route on a high-altitude buttress. Difficulties are short but sustained, and in places approach the vertical. A popular right-hand variation climbs a hanging ramp parallel to the original second pitch. Belays are potentially poor, although ice screws will help when the ice is sufficiently thick. The route is nevertheless highly recommended as an excellent and enjoyable classic. Frequently in condition after New Year.

First Ascent: R. Smith and J.R. Marshall, February 1960. Ramp variation — K.V. Crocket and C.J. Gilmore, February 1975.

Approach: As for Route 75 to the foot of Gardyloo Buttress. 1hr (plus hut approach time).

Starting Point: Below a system of grooves which cuts into the right side of the slabby front wall of the buttress.

Descent: Refer to descent notes in area introduction.

The history of the first ascent of Smith's Route is surrounded by myth. It was climbed by Smith and Marshall during a week of incredible activity on the mountain, the events of which were subsequently recorded in essays that became classics of mountain literature.

The route maintains its atmosphere of difficulty, giving high-angled ice climbing with an exposed outlook down Observatory Gully. The first pitch, which gives ice climbing throughout, begins in a corner before breaking out left on to the slabby wall. There is a possible belay in a small cave at the top of the wall, although some climbers prefer to take a hanging belay on ice below or to the left of the cave.

Depending on the amount of ice present, there is now a choice of line for the second and crucial pitch. The original line makes a rising leftward traverse before climbing directly up the fierce wall of ice above. If there is sufficient ice, the variant climbs a prominent icicle which descends from the hanging ramp above the cave. It then follows the ramp up to the left, finishing as for the original second pitch at a small rock outcrop. Finally, the easy central gully of the buttress leads to the top in about 60m.

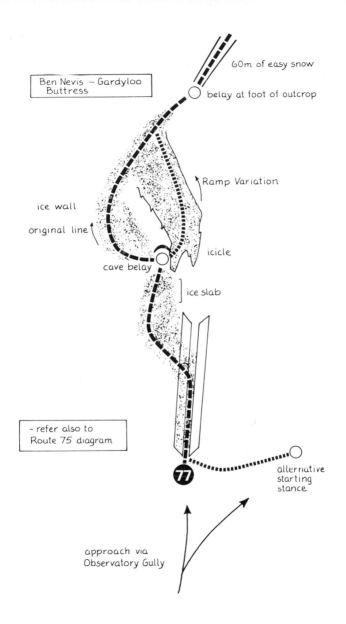

Ben Nevis – Gardyloo
Buttress

60m of easy snow

belay at foot of outcrop

Ramp Variation

ice wall

original line↑

icicle

cave belay

ice slab

– refer also to
Route 75 diagram

77

alternative
starting
stance

approach via
Observatory Gully

78: TOWER RIDGE (D) 600m

Summary: An excellent introduction to Ben Nevis, and to alpine ridge climbing. May be combined with Route 80. Although the sections of good rock climbing are infrequent, they visit positions of surprising exposure. Besides which, the Tower Gap will provide more than enough atmosphere and excitement — especially if climbed on a windy day at a time of impending darkness!

First Ascent: Refer to Route 79 (descended by J., E., B. and C. Hopkinson, September 1892).

Best Conditions: Dries quickly after rain, although one or two pitches may remain greasy on a cold day. Generally climbable from late April to October.

Approach: (1) Refer to area introduction for approaches to CIC Hut. Continue along the path above the hut, heading for scree at the foot of Observatory Gully. Round the Douglas Boulder, and continue up its east side, climbing rocks above a grassy bay, to an indeterminate hollow below the narrow East Gully. Scramble up the gully to the Douglas Gap. 30mins (plus hut approach time); or (2) approach via the Douglas Boulder Direct (Route 80).

Starting Point: At the foot of an 18m chimney which rises out of the Douglas Gap.

Descent: Refer to descent notes in area introduction.

Tower Ridge was the first rock climb to be recorded on Ben Nevis. It was climbed in descent by a family of experienced alpinists from Manchester. On the previous day they had climbed up as far as the west flank of the Great Tower, but were defeated by a steep pitch. The first ascent was made two years later by Norman Collie's party climbing in winter conditions.

From the Douglas Gap, an 18m chimney leads easily to the level crest. Where the crest steepens, a slanting ledge on the right avoids an overhanging wall. A scrambling section now intervenes, leading to the base of the Little Tower — the first steep rock step to be encountered.

The Little Tower is climbed by its left edge (steep at the top, but with good holds). A section of easy rocks now leads to the foot of the Great Tower. There is a belay at its left edge, overlooking Observatory Gully.

The next section takes the Eastern Traverse, easy but exposed. The grassy traverse ledge leads around some rocks (runner, please!) until a line leads up to a remarkable tunnel formed by a fallen block (belay). The next pitch goes through the tunnel, continuing beyond it for a few metres before striking up steep rock on good holds to the summit of the Great Tower. (At the tunnel, if time or weather is pressing, the Eastern Traverse may be used as an escape route by continuing the traverse into Observatory Gully.)

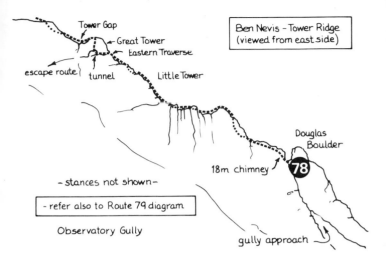

- refer also to Route 79 diagram

The top of the Great Tower is a magnificent place to be on a clear day, perched above rocks which plunge down in all directions. However, Tower Gap lies ahead and there is little time for reflection.

An incredibly narrow arete leads to a point above the Tower Gap. A block assists a safe descent into the Gap itself, from where Glover's Chimney can be seen dropping precipitously down the west side into Coire na Ciste. Good holds on the uphill side of the Gap help fend off vertigo. More importantly they lead to easier rocks and the final wall, turned on the right.

79: TOWER RIDGE IN WINTER (III) 600m +

Summary: The most amenable of the three classic winter ridges on the mountain. Major difficulties are concentrated at the Great Tower, high on the route. Spectacular views of surrounding cliffs. A few long slings and large nuts should suffice for protection and belays. Benightment awaits late starters reluctant to move together on the easier sections. Avoid a bivouac if possible, and consider retreating down the ridge if an escape by the Eastern Traverse continuation does not appeal.

First Ascent: J.N. Collie, G.A. Solly and J. Collier, March 1894.

Best Conditions: Almost any type of snow cover is suitable, excluding deep powder and other unstable conditions. Exposed to strong winds. Ascents later in the season will benefit from the extra daylight.

Approach: Refer to area introduction for approaches to CIC Hut. Ascend below the Douglas Boulder to enter the wide mouth of Observatory Gully. Now trend right (not obvious in mist) to reach the start of East Gully (*I*). Climb this to the neck between the Douglas Boulder and the start of Tower Ridge proper. 30mins (plus hut approach time). Alternatively, continue up Observatory Gully for a short distance and climb a slabby corner on the right to reach the ridge crest. This latter approach is slightly more difficult than the gully, but avoids the time-consuming chimney above the Douglas Gap.

Starting Point: According to approach.

Descent: Refer to descent notes in area introduction.

The chimney exit from the Douglas Gap can be a tough problem, but the Little Tower — climbed up the left edge on mostly good holds — presents the first real difficulties. Another long easy section leads to the foot of the Great Tower.

The Eastern Traverse beckons. It looks desperate, especially when fading into swirling mists, but in fact it proves to be relatively simple. Nevertheless, it demands caution because of its exposed and potentially dangerous position. A short ascent from its end leads to a welcome belay at a leaning block. In summer this block forms the Tunnel Route, but in winter this is often choked by snow and ice. Incidentally, if you continue the Eastern Traverse beyond the block, unlikely though this may seem, you will arrive on easy snow below Tower Gully. Worth knowing about as daylight fades with a wild night in prospect!

From just past the leaning block, the route climbs directly up the Great Tower via a difficult move in a steep corner. One final difficult pitch remains

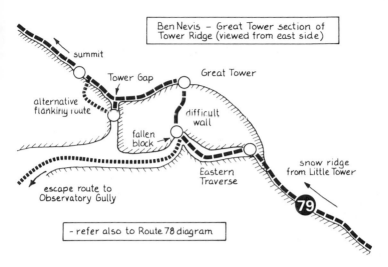

Ben Nevis – Great Tower section of Tower Ridge (viewed from east side)

summit

Tower Gap

Great Tower

alternative flanking route

difficult wall

fallen block

escape route to Observatory Gully

Eastern Traverse

snow ridge from Little Tower

79

- refer also to Route 78 diagram

— the crossing of Tower Gap. Hopefully there will be little wind as the leader teeters (crawls?) along the narrow ridge towards it. The block that once facilitated the step down disappeared a long time ago; now you must gingerly reverse on to footholds. (Hint: place a long sling before stepping down.) If things are getting desperate, one short abseil down the east side of the gap reaches snow below Tower Gully.

Once established in the gap, shudder at the drop into Glover's Chimney on the right, and without further delay climb up the steep little wall on the other side. A popular, though sometimes awkward, alternative from the gap traverses a sloping shelf on the east side of the ridge before ascending to the crest. The ridge now steepens to a belay at a wall. Now only a short rightward traverse and pleasant snow corner separate you from the plateau.

80: DOUGLAS BOULDER DIRECT (VD+) 215m

Summary: A route of surprising individuality, climbed in its own right or as a prelude to Tower Ridge (Route 78). The rock is very good, and protection excellent.

First Ascent: W. Brown, L. Hinxman, H. Raeburn and W. Douglas, April 1896.

Best Conditions: The chimney and following pitch may need 2 or 3 days to dry. Generally climbable between late April and October. 15 mins (plus hut approach time).

Approach: Refer to area introduction for approaches to CIC Hut. Leave the path just above the hut and turn right towards the Boulder.

Starting Point: Some distance up to the left of the lowest rocks, a broken, shallow groove leads to a small scoop below a chimney. Start below the groove. Alternatively, climb a pleasant rib (*VD*) which springs up from the very lowest rocks of the Boulder, and then traverse left into the scoop below the chimney (which is hidden from this approach).

Descent: From the top of the Boulder, facing Tower Ridge, go down and right a little to a block belay. Either abseil down into the Douglas Gap (leaving a large sling), or carefully down-climb a series of short grooves (*D*), avoiding steep rock by moving to the west side to land in West Gully just below the Gap. From the Gap, either continue up Tower Ridge (Route 78), or carefully descend East Gully to gain easy slopes leading rightwards (facing out) into Observatory Gully.

The first ascent party included Harold Raeburn, at the time a guest of the SMC at their Easter Meet of 1896, and Willie Douglas, editor of the Club's journal. Douglas was honoured by having the Boulder named after him.

Most parties solo the first section to the start of the chimney. This is strenuous and awkward at first, but is provided with good holds at a bulge, where a landing is effected on to the left wall. Two pitches up the chimney, which becomes more of an open groove higher up, gain a good ledge. A rightward traverse across this ledge reveals a means of progress up well-marked rocks above. These lead in several pitches to the top. Although greasy when wet, the rock and holds are excellent.

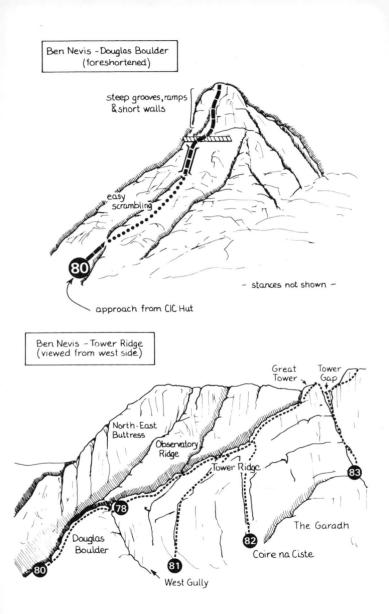

Ben Nevis - Douglas Boulder
(foreshortened)

steep grooves, ramps
& short walls

easy
scrambling

80

approach from CIC Hut

- stances not shown -

Ben Nevis - Tower Ridge
(viewed from west side)

Great
Tower

Tower
Gap

North-East
Buttress

Observatory
Ridge

Tower Ridge

83

Douglas
Boulder

78

82

The Garadh

80

81

West Gully

Coire na Ciste

81: VANISHING GULLY (V) 200m

Summary: An excellent snow and ice route, steep and sustained, with a vertical crux. Rock pegs and a good selection of screws and drive-ins required.

First Ascent: R. Marshall and G. Tiso, January 1961.

Best Conditions: Forms readily. The line is visible from the approach to the CIC Hut, and if it appears complete then an ascent could be possible. Avoid avalanche or spindrift conditions.

Approach: Refer to area introduction for approaches to CIC Hut. Ascend to the Douglas Boulder, and then follow a wide shelf under the west face of Tower Ridge, passing Douglas Gap West Gully and some grooved, broken rocks (refer to Route 84 diagram). Lean conditions expose awkward rocks on the shelf, in which case approach as for Route 82. 30mins (plus hut approach time).

Starting point: At the indefinite beginning of the slender gully line (refer to Route 80 diagram).

Descent: (1) Continue up Tower Ridge (Route 79), or, if time is short, (2) quit the route from above its final steep section, and climb up to the left to the crest of Tower Ridge. Reverse this to the Douglas Gap (possibly abseiling the chimney), and then descend East Gully into the mouth of Observatory Gully.

Thin ice adds delicacy to the first few moves, but things soon improve with some straightforward bridging at a chimney-groove. Beyond an intermediate belay, the chimney-groove leads to the main ice pitch, beneath which (in favourable conditions) you will find a cave belay. The trouble with this cave is that once safely within you won't want to leave — and with good reason: a huge, barrel-shaped ice barrier rises above. If you are lucky this will be merely vertical. Look out for protection on the right wall (there may also be a second cave).

After a final bulge, the angle suddenly eases to a more conventional belay. One more ice pitch, a bit of an imposter, brings the rocks of Secondary Tower Ridge within reach. Ice craggers now divert to Tower Ridge and an early lunch, while mountaineers stomp up the snow of a gully-ramp, arriving on Tower Ridge below the Great Tower, which of course has its own delights.

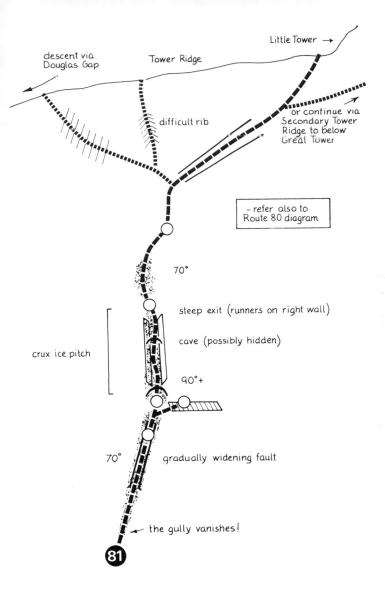

descent via Douglas Gap

Tower Ridge

Little Tower →

difficult rib

or continue via Secondary Tower Ridge to below Great Tower

– refer also to Route 80 diagram

70°

steep exit (runners on right wall)

cave (possibly hidden)

crux ice pitch

90°+

70°   gradually widening fault

← the gully vanishes!

81

82: ITALIAN CLIMB (III/IV) 180m

Summary: An easier companion climb to Vanishing, with a choice of route in the lower part. The original start may include several short pitches on 60−70 degree snow, whereas the harder right-hand variation involves 80 degree ice. Usually climbed as an interesting alternative approach to Tower Ridge.

First Ascent: Original − J.R. Marshall, A. McCorquodale and G.J. Ritchie, January 1958. Variant − S. Belk and I. Fulton, c.1970.

Best Conditions: Avoid during thaw or powder conditions, when loose snow funnels into the narrow lower section. A good build-up of snow makes the original route considerably easier, while a substantial ice build-up is required for the variation.

Approach: Refer to area introduction for approaches to CIC Hut. Now ascend into Coire na Ciste by the obvious gorge on the left side (or routes further right if conditions dictate), before traversing left under the Garadh. Refer to Route 84 diagram. 40mins (plus hut approach time).

Starting Point: At the foot of the deeply cut chimney-gully, just left of the start of Garadh Gully (refer to Route 80 diagram).

Descent: (1) Continue up Tower Ridge (Route 79) to the summit plateau, and then refer to descent notes in the area introduction, or, if time is short, (2) reverse Tower Ridge to the Douglas Gap (if necessary, abseiling the final chimney), and then descend East Gully into the mouth of Observatory Gully.

The deep chimney of the original line rises up the flanks of Tower Ridge in two or three short pitches. In lean conditions, there may be caves below the two chimney pitches, in which case the route fully deserves grade *III*. When fully banked-out, the standard may fall to grade *II*. Alternatively, divert on to an ice-fall on the right wall for two excellent pitches before rejoining the original route.

Above the pitches, a huge rock cave effectively bars the way. Avoid this on snow up to the right, and then head upwards over straightforward snow slopes. Eventually you will arrive at the crest of Tower Ridge, at a point where it is nicked by the emergence of Great Chimney − the Italian Climb's geological counterpart on the eastern flank of the ridge.

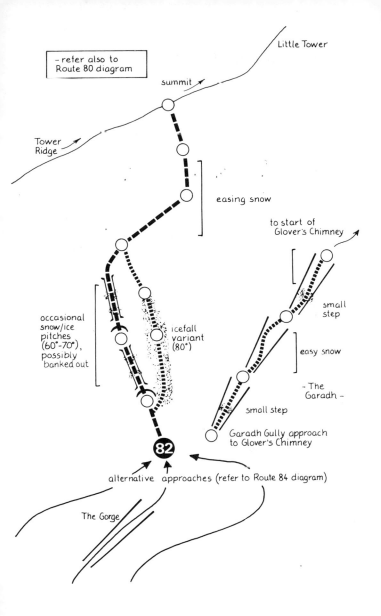

Little Tower

- refer also to
Route 80 diagram

summit

Tower Ridge

easing snow

to start of
Glover's Chimney

small step

occasional
snow/ice
pitches
(60°-70°),
possibly
banked out

icefall
variant
(80°)

easy snow

- The
Garadh -

small step

Garadh Gully approach
to Glover's Chimney

82

alternative approaches (refer to Route 84 diagram)

The Gorge

83: GLOVER'S CHIMNEY (III) 140m

Summary: A direct and position-ally grand approach to Tower Gap. Difficulties are confined to a 70 degree initial ice pitch, and a crucial chimney exit. Carry ice screws and deadmen in addition to rock protection.

First Ascent: G.G. Macphee, G.C. Williams and D. Henderson, March 1935.

Best Conditions: If the initial ice pitch is complete, and it often is, then the route is probably in condition. Conditions are never ideal in the chimney; the best one can hope for is an absence of verglas.

Approach: Refer to area intro-duction for approaches to CIC Hut. Enter Coire na Ciste by one of several lines. Under good snow cover, the obvious gorge on the left is quickest. Otherwise, ascend the outcrop to its right, starting by a small chimney. Continue up stee-pening snow, and finally traverse left to the top of the Garadh. Alternatively, traverse left below the Garadh and approach its top via Garadh Gully, which can contain anything from grade *I* to *II/III* difficulties, depending on snow cover. Refer to Route 84 diagram. 1hr (plus hut approach time).

Starting Point: At the foot of the initial ice pitch.

Descent: Continue via Tower Ridge (Route 79) to the summit plateau, then refer to descent notes in area introduction. In an emergency it would be possible to abseil from Tower Gap into Observatory Gully (avalanche risk), but in almost any circumstances it would be better to continue to the plateau.

Winter transforms the wet chimney of Glover's into an icy cleft and snow gully, guarded by a bulging ice barrier. Its ascent in these conditions sparked off the inter-war renaissance in Scottish winter climbing.

One long run-out should overcome the initial ice bulge — the first crux of the day. The long, middle section of the gully — a snow-filled channel free from significant obstacles — provides a pleasant interlude. However, this is the calm before the storm; the dreaded crux chimney lurks above. Luckily, a few flat holds on the outside of the chimney permit some inelegant bridging, although few will succeed here without a struggle. Remember to save some strength for the escape from Tower Gap!

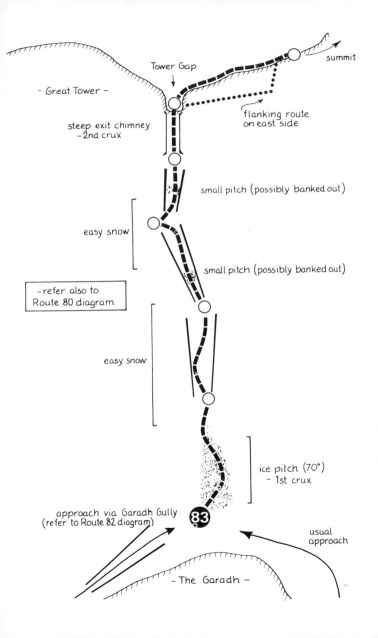

summit

Tower Gap

- Great Tower -

flanking route
on east side

steep exit chimney
- 2nd crux

small pitch (possibly banked out)

easy snow

small pitch (possibly banked out)

- refer also to
Route 80 diagram

easy snow

ice pitch (70°)
- 1st crux

approach via Garadh Gully
(refer to Route 82 diagram)

83

usual
approach

- The Garadh -

84: NUMBER TWO GULLY (II) 120m

Summary: Perhaps the most interesting of the easy Ben Nevis gullies. Ascends steepening snow between rock walls to an exciting, possibly corniced, finish. Deadmen essential.

First Ascent: J. Collier, G. Hastings and W.C. Slingsby, April 1896.

Best Conditions: A reasonable build-up of snow will suffice (the pitch will be more difficult early in the season). Avoid after heavy snowfall.

Approach: Refer to area introduction for approaches to CIC Hut. Enter Coire na Ciste by one of several lines. Under good snow cover, the obvious gorge on the left is quickest. Otherwise, ascend the outcrop to its right, starting by a small chimney. Continue up steepening snow, passing to the right of the Garadh (or climb Garadh Gully — grade *I* to *II/III*, depending on snow cover) to enter the snow-filled recess in the upper left side of the coire. 1hr (plus hut approach time).

Starting Point: At the foot of the gully (refer to diagram opposite).

Descent: Usually by No.4 Gully (refer to descent notes in area introduction).

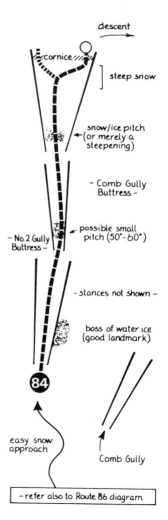

descent

cornice

steep snow

snow/ice pitch
← (or merely a
steepening)

- Comb Gully
Buttress -

possible small
← pitch (50°-60°)

- No.2 Gully
Buttress -

- stances not shown -

boss of water ice
(good landmark)

84

easy snow
approach

Comb Gully

- refer also to Route 86 diagram

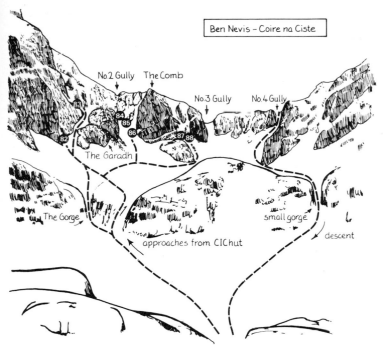

Ben Nevis – Coire na Ciste

No 2 Gully
The Comb
No.3 Gully
No.4 Gully
81
84
85
86
82
87 88
The Garadh
The Gorge
small gorge
descent
approaches from CIC hut

The first ascent of this fine little gully gave the three pioneers more than their money's worth. A late start meant that it was almost 4 pm on reaching the foot of the route. Consequently it was very cold indeed by the time they arrived below the monstrous cornice. Their fingers and toes became frost-bitten as Dr Collier tackled this formidable problem. In fact he avoided the worst of it by traversing left to exit on to a more amenable ridge.

Hastings carried his heavy brass and mahogany camera up the route — an object which had attracted much pointed comment during the ascent! Perhaps hidden away in some attic are plates of their epic climb.

85: COMB GULLY BUTTRESS (IV) 135m

Summary: A high-quality mountaineering route. Includes at least three good ice pitches in its ascent of an iced-up buttress. The original chimney finish may be avoided by a less demanding variation. Protection available from a variety of sources.

First Ascent: Original — I. Clough and J. Alexander, January 1960. Variation finish — I. Fulton and D. Gardner, January 1971.

Best Conditions: Readily comes into condition, and if anything becomes more difficult as ice accumulates.

Approach: Refer to area introduction for approaches to CIC Hut. Now approach as for Route 84 into the snow-filled recess at the upper left side of Coire na Ciste, on the left side of the Comb (pronounced as in 'cockscomb'). 1hr (plus hut approach time).

Starting Point: To the right of Number Two Gully, at the foot of a small ice-fall which is situated a little way up the right of the lowest rocks of the buttress (refer to diagram opposite).

Descent: Usually by No.4 Gully (refer to descent notes in area introduction).

The first pitch, which usually involves fifteen metres of ice set at 80 degrees or more, leads to easier climbing on the central snowfield. If the initial ice pitch is not in friendly condition, an entry to the snowfield may be possible from further up Number Two Gully.

The central snowfield leads to a fine groove on the left edge of the buttress. If thinly coated in ice, this gives an exciting exercise in technical front pointing; not too steep at 50 degrees or so, but appropriately sustained. The groove in turn leads to a belay at the foot of a short ice wall.

From here the original route, as taken by Ian Clough and John Alexander, moves right to enter a thin, right-slanting fissure. This absolutely desperate chimney may be identified from below by its black appearance, which is some indication of its lack of snow and ice. Repulsed by the original line, most parties move left to climb a short but steep ice column. This leads to a narrow, icy chimney — an exciting conclusion to an eventful route.

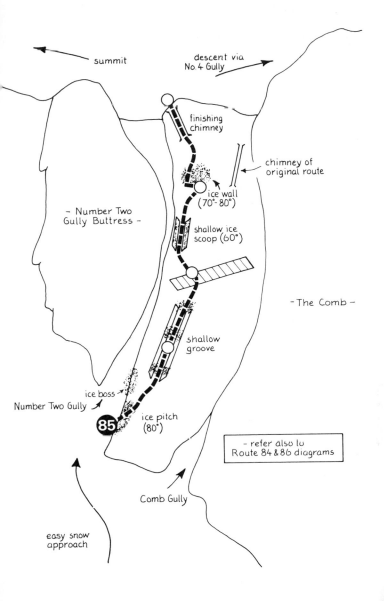

summit

descent via
No.4 Gully

finishing
chimney

chimney of
original route

ice wall
(70°-80°)

- Number Two
Gully Buttress -

shallow ice
scoop (60°)

- The Comb -

shallow
groove

ice boss

Number Two Gully

85

ice pitch
(80°)

- refer also to
Route 84 & 86 diagrams

Comb Gully

easy snow
approach

86: COMB GULLY (III/IV) 135m

Summary: A justly popular gully, with several ice pitches of increasing difficulty in the middle section. Deadmen and ice screws required (there are few peg belays).

First Ascent: F.G. Stangle, R. Morsley and P.A. Small, April 1938.

Best Conditions: Readily comes into condition, although the level of difficulty varies widely according to the quantity and quality of material (it is more variable in this respect than Green Gully). The initial section is on steep snow, and is as avalanche-prone as any snow gully.

Approach: Refer to area introduction for approaches to CIC Hut. From the hut, approach as for Route 84 to the snow-filled recess at the upper left side of Coire na Ciste. 1hr (plus hut approach time).

Starting point: At the foot of the gully, between Comb Gully Buttress and The Comb.

Descent: Usually by No.4 Gully (refer to descent notes in area introduction).

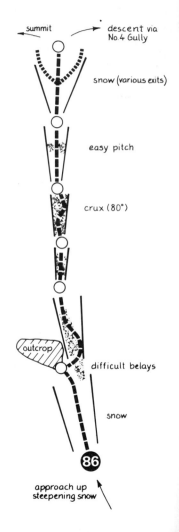

summit

descent via No.4 Gully

snow (various exits)

easy pitch

crux (80°)

outcrop

difficult belays

snow

86

approach up steepening snow

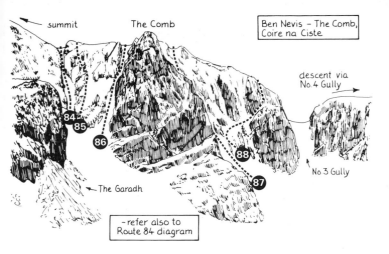

~refer also to
Route 84 diagram

Before the advent of front-pointing, Green Gully was thought more difficult than Comb Gully because its longer ice pitches were a sterner test for the skill and stamina of the step-cutting iceman. Nowadays that distinction counts for nothing, and in an average season (if there is such a thing), the climbing in Comb can be more technical.

A competent climber, encountering good snow, may solo the first section to a stance below a rock outcrop. The battered face of this wall testifies to innumerable frustrated attempts to find a good peg placement (hence the deadman).

The gully now mysteriously bends right before disappearing up a narrowing chimney. Depending on rope length and conditions, two or three pitches will eventually lead to a constricted recess tucked under a claustrophobic bulge of ice. Clearly this is going to be the crux.

On the first ascent, Stangle used a modified slater's hammer to cut holds on the crucial ice pillar. The modern front-pointer may embark on this pitch with greater panache, but risks losing composure where the ice thins out at the exit.

87: GREEN GULLY (III/IV) 120m

Summary: A classic ice route, steeped in history, and a fine companion to Comb Gully. Climbs the right flank of the Comb in four pitches. Ice sections attain 70 degrees. Deadmen, plus screws or drive-ins, required.

First Ascent: H. Raeburn and E. Phildius, April 1906.

Best Conditions: Often in condition. Poor conditions (wet snow or excessive powder) can usually be assessed from the coire, and the route avoided.

Approach: Refer to area introduction for approaches to CIC Hut. Continue the approach initially as for Route 84, into Coire na Ciste, but trend right in the upper reaches to pass below the right-hand side of the Comb on steepening snow. Refer to Route 84 diagram. 1hr (plus hut approach time).

Starting point: At the foot of the gully which bounds the Comb on its right-hand side.

Descent: Usually by No.4 Gully (refer to descent notes in area introduction).

For many years, Green Gully was the most difficult gully climb on Ben Nevis. With the passage of time, and the introduction of new techniques, it has lost some of its former glory. In lean conditions, however, or when there is a predominance of ice, it can still give of its best.

Amazing though it may seem, the magnificent first ascent of Green Gully in 1906 by Raeburn and Phildius (a Swiss gentleman on a visit to Scotland) was soon forgotten. Its achievement had never really been understood, if the truth be told, and Raeburn himself helped the process by apologising for not having succeeded in his original objective — to climb the rocks of the Comb! J.H.B. Bell attempted the gully in 1937, believing it to be unclimbed. He succeeded, and the account of this desperate second ascent is worth reading.

Modern front-pointers may be excused for overlooking Raeburn's efforts; the gully is reasonably straightforward in today's terms. However, protection is sparse and belays difficult to arrange because the rock walls, typically, are devoid of good nut or peg placements. Thankfully, there is rarely a cornice problem, and if there is, then at least one of the three possible finishes will circumvent the difficulty.

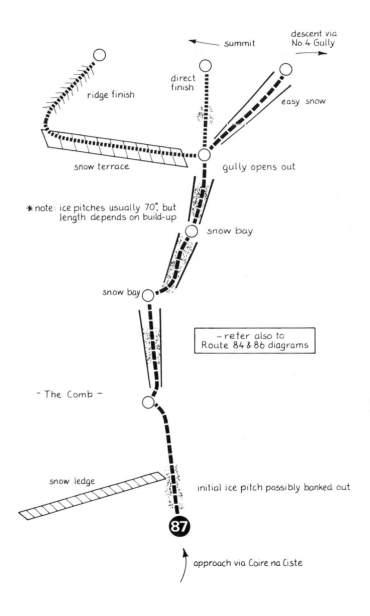

descent via
No. 4 Gully

← summit

direct
finish

ridge finish

easy snow

snow terrace

gully opens out

✳ note: ice pitches usually 70°, but
length depends on build-up

snow bay

snow bay

– refer also to
Route 84 & 86 diagrams

– The Comb –

snow ledge

initial ice pitch possibly banked out

87

↑ approach via Coire na Ciste

88: NUMBER THREE GULLY BUTTRESS (III) 120m

Summary: One of the most entertaining buttress climbs on the mountain. A varied approach on snow and ice leads to an unlikely and exhilarating climax. Exposed but well protected. Good rock protection on the upper section, but carry a deadman for the initial pitches.

First Ascent: L.S. Lovat and D. Bennet, February 1957.

Best Conditions: Firm snow is preferable for the snowfield traverse.

Approach: Refer to area introduction for approaches to CIC Hut. Continue the approach initially as for Route 84, into Coire na Ciste, but trend right in the upper reaches to pass below the right-hand side of the Comb on steepening snow. Refer to Route 84 diagram. 1hr (plus hut approach time).

Starting Point: At the foot of slabby rocks, just right of the start of Green Gully, from where a large snow ledge which runs across the lower part of the buttress may be accessed.

Descent: Usually by No.4 Gully (refer to descent notes in area introduction).

The first ascent of the original route in summer resulted from an abortive attempt by Raeburn and the Inglis Clarks on Green Gully (a repulsive *V. Diff.* in summer). The climb amply compensated their efforts. Three Gully Buttress has since become a firm favourite, especially when winter transforms its moderate rocks into a route of alpine character.

The initial slabs can be a little too exciting if thinly iced, but normally the cover is sufficient to dispel worries. Once established on the big snow ledge, the route proceeds by a rising traverse to the right. A good stance is reached at the high point of the ledge, below and to the right of an icy corner which cuts through the upper buttress.

From this secure niche, the climbing becomes *really* exciting! An unlikely sequence begins with a rightward traverse and some upward moves to gain a large platform. From here an obvious traverse ledge leads out to the right, across the buttress, to a belay at its far end; enjoyable and safe climbing in a good situation — the best of mixtures. One more pitch up iced slabs leads to the top.

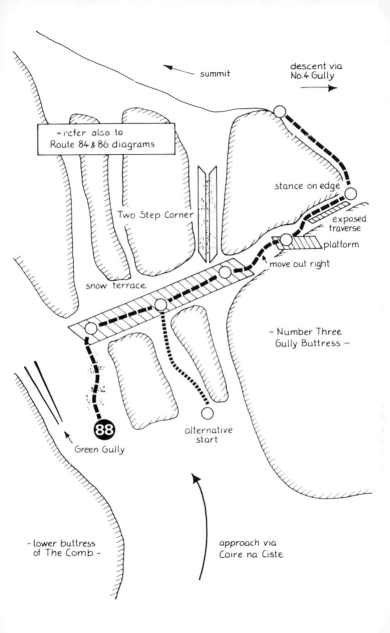

89: THE CURTAIN (IV) 110m

Summary: An excellent route of surprising interest. Very popular. Climbs the left side of Carn Dearg Buttress in three sustained ice pitches. The diligent will find good belays and adequate protection. Nuts and a selection of screws and drive-ins required.

First Ascent: J. Knight and D. Bathgate, February 1965.

Best Conditions: Quickly comes into condition, but readily falls down during a thaw − try to be somewhere else when it does! If the first 20m of iced slab are climbable, then the remainder of the route should also be possible.

Approach: Refer to area introduction for approaches to CIC Hut. From the hut, ascend towards No.5 Gully (avalanche-prone), then traverse rightwards to the foot of the obvious icy slab. 20mins (plus hut approach time).

Starting Point: Below the right-hand corner of the slab (peg or nut belay on the right).

Descent: Descend leftwards via the large sloping terrace to enter No.5 Gully (take care in bad snow conditions).

This is probably the busiest Grade *IV* in the country. Sometimes a strange, indented feature will form in the first pitch − a groove worn down by the passage of countless crampons. Despite this indignity, the route is well worth doing, particularly during late afternoon when the crowds have gone (but don't forget the headtorch).

The first pitch introduces the climb gently; easy on the arms, and with the prospect of a couple of screw runners (there is also an old peg on the right wall, missed by many). Climb until the rope runs out, and then occupy a troglodyte stance in a tiny cave.

The crux pitch climbs the bulge above the cave in a sinuous line. This can be awkward, and the tendency is to rush. An exposed but secure stance rewards the patient.

Time to switch on the headtorch as you swing rightwards to start the final pitch. An initial convex bulge conceals a modest finishing slab − an echo of the first. Each blow of the pick gives birth to a cascade of minute ice spicules in the beam of light − a display unseen in daytime. At the terrace you can sit in the snow and be content.

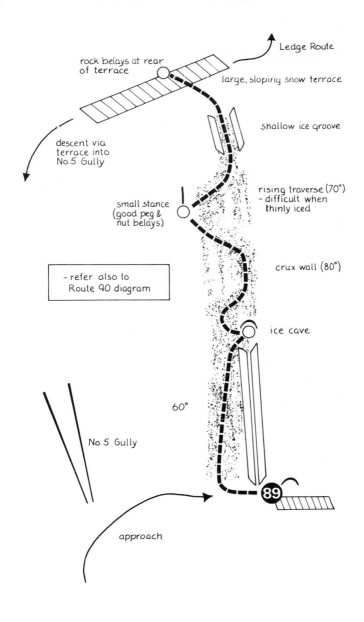

Ledge Route

rock belays at rear
of terrace

large, sloping snow terrace

shallow ice groove

descent via
terrace into
No.5 Gully

rising traverse (70°)
– difficult when
thinly iced

small stance
(good peg &
nut belays)

– refer also to
Route 90 diagram

crux wall (80°)

ice cave

60°

No.5 Gully

89

approach

90: ROUTE II (S) 150m

Summary: The route cuts boldly across *Very Severe* territory, visiting unusually exciting positions for the grade. Rough slabs of excellent rock temper the unremitting exposure.

First Ascent: Original route — B.P. Kellett and W.A. Russell, June 1943. Direct Start — B.W. Robertson and G. Chisholm, May 1962.

Best Conditions: Allow 2 to 3 days to dry after rain. Normally climbable from late April through to October.

Approach: Refer to area introduction for approaches to CIC Hut. Ascend easy ground to gain the foot of Carn Dearg Buttress. 20mins (plus hut approach time).

Starting Point: At the foot of a lesser, curving buttress of clean, grey rock which lies on the lower left flank of the main buttress.

Descent: From the platform at the top of the climb, go left and descend via Ledge Route (*E*) into the lower reaches of No.5 Gully. Descend this easily to the foot of the Buttress.

Brian Kellett was an enigmatic character who lived below Ben Nevis in the summers of 1943 and 1944. When unable to find a partner, he would often climb solo. He was killed in September 1944, while roped to a companion. By then he had climbed most of the existing routes on the mountain, and had recorded 32 first ascents.

Kellett had appeared at the door of the CIC Hut looking for a partner. A student party was in residence and Arnot Russell, their best climber, agreed to go along. Despite the light rain, the two men were rewarded with the first ascent of this remarkably fine *Severe*.

Their route utilised the start of a Route I. However, the later Direct Start adds 75m of independent climbing, beginning up the centre of a smooth slab. It rejoins the original route after three pitches, at a belay near a prominent chimney — the line of Route I.

The next pitch follows the chimney for 12m, but then breaks out right to a belay at the start of a long, rising traverse below the great overhangs of the buttress. This ultimately leads to a platform on the buttress edge, from where a groove leads up to easier rock on its crest.

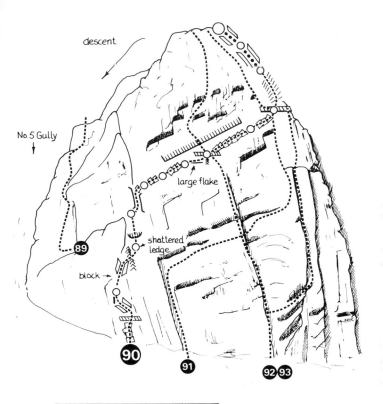

descent

No 5 Gully

89

block →

shattered
ledge

large flake

90

91

92 93

Ben Nevis - Carn Dearg Buttress
(foreshortened)
- refer also to Route 91 diagram -

91: THE BULLROAR (HVS) 250m

Summary: A sustained and serious climb which traverses the great central slabs of the buttress in a position of constant exposure. Retreat from the traverse could prove difficult. Exposed moves on the second slab pitch constitute the technical crux.

First Ascent: J.R. Marshall and J. Stenhouse, May 1961.

Best Conditions: Allow 2 to 3 days to dry after rain. Best climbed early rather than late in the day, as a wet streak often develops on the crux slab in the late afternoon. Climbable from late April to October.

Approach: As for Route 90.

Starting Point: At some large boulders below the left-hand section of the buttress.

Descent: As for Route 90.

The Bullroar was probably the finest summer climb recorded on Ben Nevis by J.R. Marshall, its supreme expert, rivalling Minus One Direct as the best route on the mountain. Bold in concept, its subtle line was a masterpiece in route-finding.

The name derives from the '*bullroar*' used by Australian Aborigines – a wooden slat whirled on a rope to produce a roaring sound during the initiation rites of young men. Its echo greets those who, by succeeding on this climb, complete their initiation to this great buttress.

The first few moves, in a steep and strenuous groove, also include some of the hardest. Originally a peg was used here, but the route is now free. The next pitch takes a parallel groove on the left, leading to a belay before the start of the great traverse pitches.

The crux comes on the second of them: a descent and traverse to a thin crack (peg runner usually in place – back rope for second advisable). This is followed by another short but delicate descent, leading to moves right and a stance above an overlap.

The traverse across the vast slab continues in an impressive situation to a belay above the third pitch of Centurion. It ends two pitches later at a terrace on the buttress edge. Thereafter the route moves left to an undercut groove, and then makes a bid for the top via this and the corners and slabby grooves which follow.

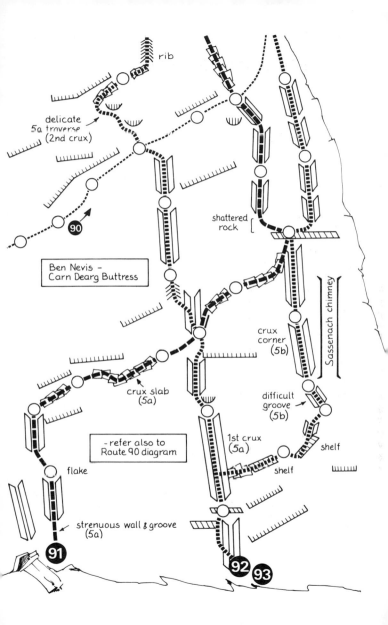

rib

delicate
5a traverse
(2nd crux)

90

Ben Nevis -
Carn Dearg Buttress

shattered
rock

Sassenach chimney

crux slab
(5a)

crux
corner
(5b)

difficult
groove
(5b)

- refer also to
Route 90 diagram

1st crux
(5a)

shelf

shelf

flake

strenuous wall & groove
(5a)

91

92 93

92: CENTURION (HVS) 215m

Summary: One of the major rock climbs in the country. Takes the buttress directly, via a great corner, to find an improbable exit through the overhangs above. (Illustrated on Route 91 diagram.)

First Ascent: D.D. Whillans and R.O. Downes, August 1956.

Best Conditions: Allow 2 to 3 fine days after rain, perhaps longer after prolonged bad weather. Generally climbable between late April and October.

Approach: As for Route 90.

Starting Point: Below the huge, open-book corner which cuts upwards through the centre of the buttress.

Descent: As for Route 90.

To the complacent Scots, the ascent of Centurion by the English rope of Whillans and Downes was a national disaster. It had been attempted several times by home teams, but without urgency or success. The big second pitch occupied Whillans for some time, while the amazing sixth pitch through the overhangs was led by Bob Downes (who was shortly to die on Masherbrum).

The first pitch climbs the deceptive left wall of the undercut groove, before moving right and up the groove to a ledge. The first crux looms up ahead in the steep corner. This is well protected, however, and the rock generally friendly. It leads to a belay on a slab below an overhang.

The next section begins up easy grooves on the left, before moving rightwards on to the lip of an overhang. This is followed by a pitch up the corner, left wall, and arete. Two easy pitches up slabby grooves then lead to the overhangs which dominate the upper section of the buttress.

The second crux lies above: up to the overhang; left to an inclined slab; up left to a second overhang; and then up left again from a detached flake, delicately, to gain a large slab below a second series of bulges. Finally, a rib and bulge right of the stance lead to a finish up an easy groove.

To a tired leader, the final bulging arete may be found strenuous, but the difficulties are short. Technically, the early moves on the sixth pitch are probably as hard as any, whereas the huge second pitch corner can be tiring.

93: THE BAT (E2) 300m

Summary: A classic hard route by two of Scotland's best-known mountaineers. A traverse right from the foot of the Centurion corner gains the main feature of the route — the hanging corner. Difficult climbing in the lower reaches climaxes at this corner, with the strenuous and uncompromising ascent of its steep crack and roof. (Illustrated on Route 91 diagram.)

First Ascent: D. Haston and R. Smith, September 1959.

Best Conditions: Allow 2 to 3 days to dry after rain. Generally climbable between late April and October.

Approach: As for Route 90.

Starting Point: As for Centurion, below the huge, open-book corner which cuts up through the centre of the buttress.

Descent: As for Route 90.

The ascent of The Bat gave Ben Nevis its hardest summer line for many years, and inspired Robin Smith to write his famous essay, *The Bat and the Wicked*. The first ascent came after several unsuccessful attempts, and used some aid on the mossy and slimy crux pitch. Both climbers sustained falls here, held by a peg placed at the roof. Present-day climbers will gratefully clip this peg for a runner.

The main pitch is reached by some devious route-finding. From 10m up the second pitch of Centurion, it traverses out right on slabs to a block. A shelf continues the line to a block belay, beyond which a short descent gains another shelf leading up and right into a corner. A short wall, slab, and V-groove precede moves right across slabs to a belay under the Sassenach chimney.

The next two pitches are hard. The very steep groove beyond the left edge leads to the crux corner (belay on a little slab below the corner). The corner is climbed direct via a crack, roof, and continuation crack, to a gradual easing. The pitch calls on a variety of jamming and bridging techniques, as well as hidden reserves of strength. The remainder of the climb, based on a series of grooves, is thankfully easier.

Creag Meaghaidh Area

Winter climbs on the Coire Ardair flank of Creag Meaghaidh (pronounced 'Meggie') are among the best in Scotland. They are much easier to protect than comparable routes on Ben Nevis, thanks to the schistose rock which provides many cracks for pegs. The cliffs come into condition relatively quickly after heavy snowfall, but are prone to rapid thaw. Good conditions are difficult to predict.

The routes finish on a great, featureless plateau. The mountain lacks a summit shelter, so this is no place to linger in bad conditions — carry a map and compass. The rock on Meaghaidh does not lend itself to summer climbing. In contrast, the metamorphic rock of Binnein Shuas is excellent.

It is worth mentioning that the conservation movement barely succeeded in preventing afforestation of the lower slopes of Creag Meaghaidh, despite the area's designation as a 'Site of Special Scientific Interest'. Clearly, all hill-users will want to take extra care here, as elsewhere, to preserve the environment.

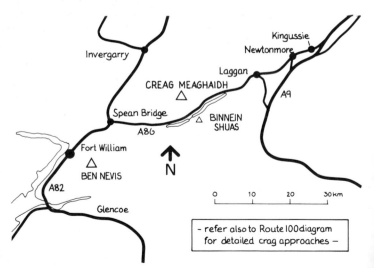

- refer also to Route 100 diagram for detailed crag approaches —

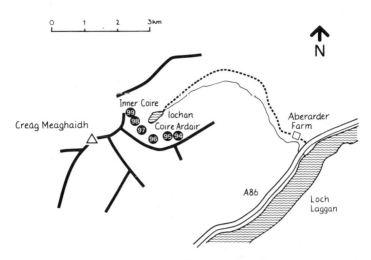

Approaches: Approach by the A9 when travelling from southern Scotland, and then turn left on the A889. This leads, via Dalwhinnie, to a junction with the A86 Spean Bridge – Newtonmore road. Turn left towards Spean Bridge to locate the approach walks for both Meaghaidh and Binnein Shuas. From Fort William, approach by the A82 to Spean Bridge, and then follow the A86 towards Newtonmore. The nearest railway station is at Tulloch on the A86, 15km west of Aberarder.

Accommodation: No single centre serves this area. Hotels can be found in villages in both directions along the Spean Bridge – Laggan – Newtonmore road. Camping near Aberarder Farm is discouraged. Climbing huts in the area include the JMCS (Edinburgh) hut at Jock's Spot, just south of Creag Dubh, Newtonmore, and the luxurious new SMC Raeburn Hut on the A889 between Dalwhinnie and Laggan at GR:636 908 (book via your club secretary). For Binnein Shuas, good camping may be had around Lochan na h-Earba (except in the stalking season).

Stuart Smith on Smith's Gully (Route 94), Creag Meaghaidh.
(Photo: Colin Stead)

Alan Pettit on the first pitch of South Post Direct (Route 96), Creag Meaghaidh. (Photo: Colin Stead)

94: SMITH'S GULLY (V) 180m

Summary: One of the best gully climbs in the country. It has a fierce reputation, not least because it is often out of condition and is frequently swept by powder avalanches. Includes at least five good pitches, mostly on ice, at angles of up to 90 degrees. Rock pegs and a good selection of screws and drive-ins required (including Warthog-type drive-ins for frozen turf).

First Ascent: J.R. Marshall and G. Tiso, February 1959.

Best Conditions: Creag Meaghaidh comes into condition relatively quickly after heavy snowfall. However, it is susceptible to rapid thaw, which makes conditions difficult to predict. Given a good build-up, a settled spell of cold weather should give the best chance on this route.

Approach: Park by the A86, and walk up the road to Aberarder Farm (GR:483 875). Continue by the path behind the farm, west then north-west, above the Allt Coire Ardair. The rising path gradually bends to the south-west to reveal the superb frontage of cliffs. Continue to Lochan a'Choire Ardair. Refer to the diagram opposite, and ascend Raeburn's Gully towards the three prominent gully lines at the left side of Pinnacle Buttress (GR:418 875). 2hrs 30mins (unless delayed by deep snow).

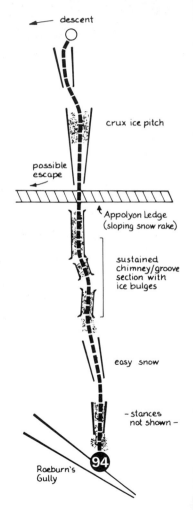

descent

crux ice pitch

possible escape

Appolyon Ledge (sloping snow rake)

sustained chimney/groove section with ice bulges

easy snow

– stances not shown –

94

Raeburn's Gully

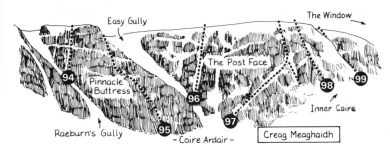

Starting Point: At the foot of the central gully line.

Descent: (1) If conditions and visibility are good, go left from the finish and descend by Raeburn's Gully (*I*). (2) In poor conditions, descend by Sron a'Choire as for Route 95.

Jimmy Marshall was fast approaching the peak of his form during the winter of 1959. Following his fine ascents of Smith's Gully (named in recognition of an earlier attempt by Robin Smith, which had foundered in poor conditions), and 1959 Face Route, he went on to Ben Nevis to make the first ascent of another major classic — Minus Two Gully.

The first section of the gully involves sustained chimneys and grooves, and one short section of snow. The last steep pitch leads out to a temporary easing of the angle, where a prominent shelf runs across the face. The shelf is Appolyon Ledge (*II*), which is used by the girdle traverse. It also provides, if necessary, a leftward escape from this route, crossing Ritchie's Gully (*IV*) into Raeburn's Gully.

The crux pitch rises above the shelf, its icy bulges forming the last major barrier before the final easing. The strong and confident will front-point indiscriminately up the pitch, while those weakened by the campaign may find it helpful to stay in a faint groove on the left. All will be rewarded by straightforward snow leading to the plateau.

95: 1959 FACE ROUTE (IV) 450m

Summary: One of the longest and most entertaining mixed buttress routes in the country. Climbs ice, snow, rock, and frozen turf, in a variety of exciting and impressive situations. A route for the connoisseur. Ice protection and rock pegs required.

First Ascent: J.R. Marshall, J. Stenhouse and D. Haston, February 1959.

Best Conditions: Snowfall followed by a good freeze should bring this great face into condition. Wait for substantial cover and plenty of daylight.

Approach: As for Route 94.

Starting Point: Just right of the lowest rocks of Pinnacle Buttress, below an obvious depression which slants up to the left.

Descent: (1) In good conditions, go right from the finish to descend by Easy Gully (*I*). The steepest section is in the middle, but should not exceed about 40 degrees. (2) In poor conditions, go left and then walk eastwards along the ridge to the top of Sron a'Choire. Descend its east ridge to Aberarder Farm (footbridge across the burn near the farm).

The rock of Creag Meaghaidh is a fissile mica schist, forming vegetatious and loose walls in summer (when it is worthless for rock climbing). However, in winter it provides icy smears and frozen turf, plus some rock belays. This route makes good use of these properties as it seeks out a series of shallow gullies and grooves in the face, and alternates them with traverses and ice-falls. The route-finding is immensely enjoyable.

The initial depression shades into a shallow gully, then an icy chimney. The route follows this line for about 60m before heading leftwards, for a further 60m, to gain the base of a left-raking chimney-groove (obvious chockstone). The groove leads in 90m to large snow ledges in the middle of the buttress.

From the snow ledges, another gully will be seen to the right of the imposing summit tower, trending leftward to a finish about 60m below the top of the buttress. The base of this gully is often barred by an impressive ice-fall. It has been climbed, but may be turned on the right by a rock wall.

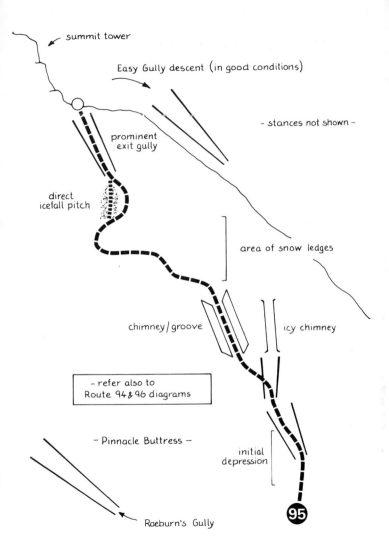

summit tower

Easy Gully descent (in good conditions)

prominent
exit gully

- stances not shown -

direct
icefall pitch

area of snow ledges

chimney / groove

icy chimney

- refer also to
Route 94 & 96 diagrams

- Pinnacle Buttress -

initial
depression

95

Raeburn's Gully

96: THE SOUTH POST (III or IV) 400m

Summary: A fine snow and ice climb, ascending a prominent gully on the Post Face. Bypassing the two ice pitches of the Direct reduces the overall grade to *III*. Deadmen required in addition to screws and drive-ins.

First Ascent: Original route — N.S. Tennent and C.G.M. Slesser, February 1956. Pitch One direct — T.W. Patey and F.R. Brooke, March 1962. Pitch Three direct — I.A. MacEacheran and J. Knight, March 1964.

Best Conditions: Readily comes into condition. Avoid sunny days later in the season — the Post Face catches the sun and is liable to avalanche.

Approach: As for Route 94 to the lochan. Centre Post rises from just above the foot of Easy Gully; South Post starts a little further up the gully.

Starting Point: Original — at the foot of Centre Post. Direct — below the steep ice pillar of the main gully line.

Descent: (1) In good conditions, go left and descend Easy Gully (*I*). The steepest section is in the middle, but should not exceed about 40 degrees. (2) In poor conditions, descend by Sron a'Choire as for Route 95.

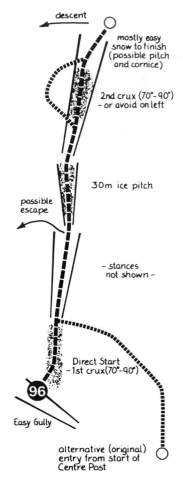

descent

mostly easy snow to finish (possible pitch and cornice)

2nd crux (70°-90°) - or avoid on left

30m ice pitch

possible escape

- stances not shown -

Direct Start - 1st crux (70°-90°)

96

Easy Gully

alternative (original) entry from start of Centre Post

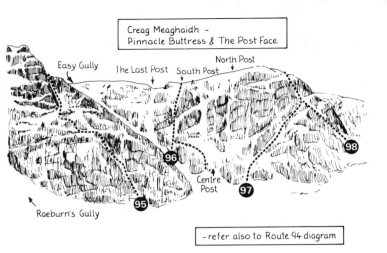

- refer also to Route 94 diagram

South Post provides an immensely enjoyable bout of front-pointing when in good condition. When climbed by the Direct, at grade *IV*, the route includes two ice pitches angled at 70 to 90 degrees. There may also be an intermediate ice pitch, as well as cornice difficulties at the exit.

The buttress between South Post and Centre Post — the Central Pillar — has a small snowfield about 20m above Easy Gully. On the Original, this snowfield is reached by climbing steeply up to the left from below the start of the Centre Post. This line then leads leftward to enter the South Post itself, just above its Direct Start (which almost banks out in some winters).

A couloir rises above the Direct's initial pitch. It may contain a 30m ice pitch in a good winter. Above this the gully narrows and rears up in the crux ice-fall of the Direct. This can be avoided on the left, re-entering the gully higher up, but there will be one small pitch to overcome before gaining the plateau.

97: STAGHORN GULLY (III) 450m

Summary: A subtle and comparatively safe line. Deservedly popular. The Original Start involves exposed traversing on snow, but there is an optional Direct Start at grade *IV*. Deadmen required in addition to screws and drive-ins.

First Ascent: C.M. Allan, J.H.B. Bell, H.M. Kelly and H. Cooper, April 1934.

Best Conditions: Often in condition.

Approach: As for Route 94 to the lochan. Now head towards the right-hand end of the Post Face.

Staghorn Gully takes the line of a shelf which slants up to the right, across the massive boundary wall between the Post Face and the Inner Coire.

Starting Point: Start at the foot of the shelf, just right of the North Post.

Descent: (1) In good conditions, go left and descend Easy Gully (*I*). The steepest section is in the middle, but should not exceed about 40 degrees. (2) In poor conditions, descend by Sron a'Choire as for Route 95.

Staghorn Gully can be a useful route when the steeper snow slopes are in a dubious condition. Initially it crosses the massive, sprawling buttress with five or so rope lengths on snow (the line is partly obscured from below, and not to be confused with a higher, interrupted ledge). This exposed traverse of the shelf leads to parallel chimney-gullies separated by a narrow rock pillar. The right-hand line − the North Pipe − provides enjoyable climbing over several short ice steps, leading to a small snow bowl below the plateau. The difficult left-hand line − the South Pipe − has a grade *IV* Direct Start up a shallow gully. This may equally well be used as a direct approach to the North Pipe.

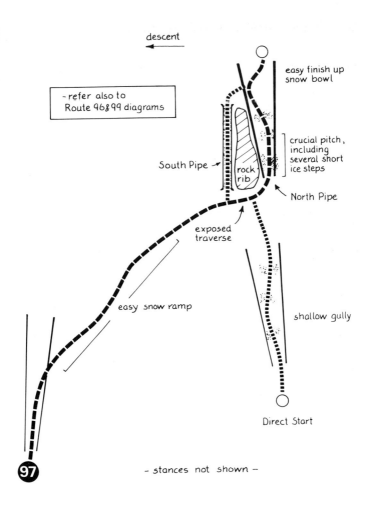

descent

- refer also to
Route 96 & 99 diagrams

easy finish up
snow bowl

crucial pitch,
including
several short
ice steps

South Pipe

rock
rib

North Pipe

exposed
traverse

easy snow ramp

shallow gully

Direct Start

97

- stances not shown -

98: THE PUMPKIN (IV/V) 300m

Summary: Yet another good ice route. Ascends the left-hand side of the Inner Coire face. Well protected with ice screws. Deadmen and rock pegs required for belays.

First Ascent: R. McMillan, G.S. Peet and N. Quinn, April 1968.

Best Conditions: Frequently in condition. Viability can be assessed from the approach.

Approach: As for Route 94 to the lochan. Now trend rightwards, passing the Post Face, towards the Inner Coire.

Starting Point: Below the obvious ice corner (refer to Route 99 diagram).

Descent: From the finish, turn right and descend north towards an obvious col known as the Window. Descend easily via this into Coire Ardair.

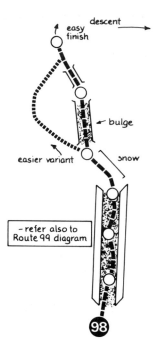

The Pumpkin starts unequivocally with 90m of ice, the centre section of which bulges. Two or three pitches of this lead to a short length of snow. Here a shark's fin of rock descends from above, splitting the line and providing a choice of route. The normal finish takes the fine chimney-gully on the right. It may include an awkward bulge. If in poor condition (route or party!), the slanting line to the left of the fin provides an easier alternative. Either way, the top will be gained by easy climbing above the fin.

99: CINDERELLA (I/II) 200m

Summary: A pleasant and straightforward snow ascent in the centre of the Inner Coire face. Deadmen required.

First Ascent: T.W. Patey and W. Tout, February 1963.

Best Conditions: A reasonable snowfall should render this route climbable. It may contain one or two small ice pitches early in the season. Avoid thaw conditions.

Approach: As for Route 94 to the lochan. Now head towards the Inner Coire. Cinderella is the obvious snow gully which cuts up through the middle of the cliffs of the Inner Coire, about half-way between The Pumpkin and the right-hand end of the cliffs.

Starting Point: At the foot of the gully.

Descent: From the finish, turn right and descend north towards an obvious col known as the Window. Descend easily via this into Coire Ardair.

On a sunny winter's morning, the approach walk to Lochan a'Choire Ardair is a pleasure in itself. Initially the Pinnacle Face and Post Face dominate the view, and only on passing into the Inner Coire are the secrets of its cliff revealed. Cinderella, the gentle waif of the coire, has no nasty shocks in store. In providing a straightforward route to the summit plateau, it serves as a fine introduction to the winter climbs of Creag Meaghaidh.

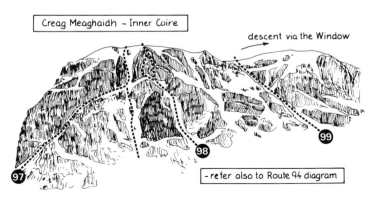

Creag Meaghaidh - Inner Coire

descent via the Window

97   98   99

- refer also to Route 94 diagram

100: ARDVERIKIE WALL (S) 165m

Summary: A delightful climb in a delightful setting, navigating a sea of slabs on friendly rock. After the initial pitch, the route follows the wall more or less directly, although the actual line may be varied at will. Belays and protection are good.

First Ascent: D.F. Lang and G.N. Hunter, June 1967.

Best Conditions: The crag receives less rainfall than most, but when wet the metamorphic rock becomes greasy due to a very thin film of lichen. Access is restricted from mid-August through October by stalking.

Approach: From a concrete bridge (GR:433 830) on the A86 Spean Bridge to Newtonmore road, about 1km west of Loch Laggan. Cross the bridge and follow the track, going left at the first fork and passing a locked gate. At the next fork, take the narrower track to the right, climbing gently round the south-west flank of Binnein Shuas, to reach Lochan na h-Earba. The cliffs are now visible to the west of the lochan. 1hr 20mins.

Starting Point: The cliff is split into west and east sectors by Hidden Gully (not visible from the

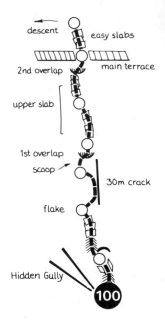

approach). The route takes the right wall of the gully, starting below a rib, 8m left of a boulder arch.

Descent: Go left, and descend the ridge above the west sector to easy ground. This in turn leads down to the base of the cliff.

12 . 6 . 93
K Fullerton
C. Brown
M. Lock

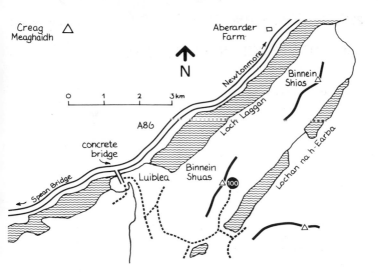

At first sight, Ardverikie Wall does not appear particularly impressive. The crag hides its true features from this distance. On approach, the leviathan wall looms overhead and the pulse quickens. A *Severe* leader might quake at the sight; but be reassured, the clean rock is rough and delightfully secure.

The first pitch follows a rib and corner to a niche. From here the line returns to the rib on the left, and continues by a slab, climbing this first right and then left to a flake belay.

The second pitch moves right from the flake to follow a magnificent 30m crack — the central feature of the wall, and the heart of the climb. Linger and enjoy, because all too soon it leads to a belay below a scoop.

The third pitch climbs the left side of the scoop before crossing an overlap to gain the upper slab. This is climbed more or less directly in two pitches, breaking through a second overlap just below the terrace. Easy slabs above the terrace put an end to the climbing, and to this book. A pity — if only it could go on for ever (the climbing, that is . . .).

Also in the Crowood Classic Climbs series:

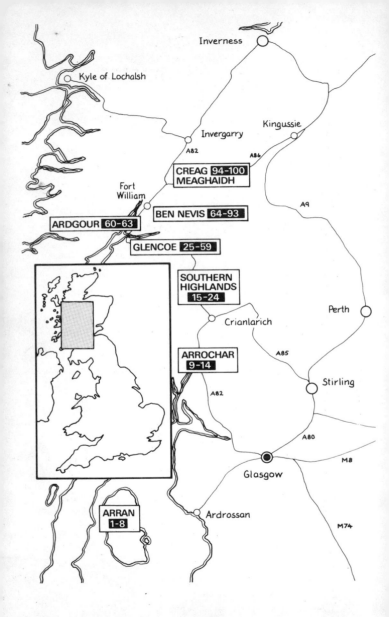

Inverness

Kyle of Lochalsh

Kingussie

Invergarry
A82   A86

CREAG 94-100
MEAGHAIDH

A9

Fort
William

BEN NEVIS 64-93

ARDGOUR 60-63

GLENCOE 25-59

SOUTHERN
HIGHLANDS
15-24

Perth

Crianlarich

ARROCHAR
9-14

A85

A82

Stirling

A80

M8

Glasgow

Ardrossan

M74

ARRAN
1-8